Real Crime

Real Crime

Four crimes that shocked a nation

SHARI-JAYNE BODA

GRANADA

First published in Great Britain in 2003
By Granada Media, an imprint of Andre Deutsch Limited
20 Mortimer Street
London W1T 3JW

A catalogue record is available from the British Library

ISBN 0 233 00002 X

Typeset by E-Type, Liverpool

Printed and bound in Great Britain

2 4 6 8 10 9 7 5 3 1

CONTENTS

Introduction 9

The Heiress and the Kidnapper 16

Jeremy Bamber 73

Kenneth Noye: A Face from the Past 136

Girlsnatcher 198

INTRODUCTION

Maybe it's because I grew up in a town that was home to *Z Cars* that I have a particular interest in the relationship between crime and television. The sprawling council estate of Kirkby, near Liverpool, provided the backdrop for Britain's favourite cop show in the 1960s and '70s. Some said Kirkby suffered because of its *Z Cars* image, but to me the weekly diet of petty crime seemed pretty tame compared to what you could actually witness out on the street after the pubs closed. If anything, I felt *Z Cars* added a splash of colour to a landscape featuring too many grey tower blocks, empty houses and shops with metal grilles on the windows. There we were every Monday night, on the BBC, our shops, our churches, our pubs, our homes, with opening titles featuring faces of people we knew. For me, the link between crime and television was firmly established.

Black-and-white TV boasted not only *Z Cars*. There was *Softly, Softly*, featuring the unforgettable Barlow (Stratford Johns) and Watt (Frank Windsor); the French detective *Maigret* with its unmistakeable theme tune and, of course, George Dixon (Jack Warner) in *Dixon of Dock Green*. Late at night, you could watch *Gideon's Way*, starring John Gregson, Elliot Ness and The Untouchables, and my all-time favourite – and probably the single biggest influence on the *Real Crime* series – *Scotland Yard Casebook*, presented from a large armchair by the incomparable Edgar Lustgarten.

Scotland Yard Casebook was a mixture of documentary and drama – what television executives today call a 'drama-doc'. Made between 1953 and 1961 for the cinema, it transferred to television and always began with Edgar Lustgarten's straight, no-nonsense introduction allowing viewers to begin at the beginning, with a brief resume of what the audience needed to know. He then spoke out of vision as stiff-backed actors played out the opening scenes. These were real-life cases from the annals of Scotland Yard. Murder, robbery, fraud, kidnap – all thoughtfully told and dramatised, and all had a twist in the tale to keep you watching after midnight.

When I joined ITV in 1998 as a controller of news and current affairs, I told producers I wanted ideas for a new crime programme with the hallmark values of *Scotland Yard Casebook*. This completely mystified most of them because they were so young they had never heard of it. So I patiently explained, saddened that so much budding, promising talent lived in ignorance of Edgar Lustgarten, that I wanted a programme that featured iconic cases, the highest production values, a clear narrative and – crucially – something new to say. It wouldn't be enough to revisit an old, well-worn case and dress it up with fancy filming. Each programme had to leave viewers saying: 'I thought I knew all about this case. Now I realise I didn't know the half of it.'

My boss at ITV, David Liddiment, gave his support to a special two-part documentary on the Krays, made by Frank Simmonds of Carlton Television. This featured, for the first time, the only known colour footage of Ronnie and Reggie in their heyday. Interviews with former Kray henchmen Albert Donoghue and Freddie Foreman also took viewers inside the twins' empire. Foreman's admission on TV that he had actually committed a murder for which he had been acquitted led to questions in the House of Commons and a revision of the law on 'double jeopardy'. Ratings for the two programmes surpassed expectations, with seven million viewers. The template for ITV's new crime show had been set.

But what to call it? Because I wanted to concentrate on cases the public were familiar with, I toyed with the title *Front Page Crime*, but rejected it because it felt like the sort of title journalists would like but the public would not. The decision, in the end, was embarrassingly simple and mundane. In the summer of 1999, ITV began broadcasting a new documentary series titled *Real Life*. Over lunch with the series editor, Stephen Lambert of RDF Television, the title came to me – *Real Crime*. OK, I won't pretend any of this is rocket science, and you may argue that 'Real Crime' actually doesn't really mean anything. What, after all, is an Unreal Crime? But the title had a ring to it and I liked it. So did the boss. *Real Crime* was born.

The first series began on ITV at 10.30pm on Wednesday, June 6, 2001. Directed by James Strong, and produced by Jane Beacon and Sarah Caplin of Granada Television, 'The Hunt for Wearside Jack' was an investigation into the infamous 'I'm Jack' tape that wrong-footed the police for more than two years in their hunt for the Yorkshire Ripper. It was a drama-doc, with Martin Pearson playing the part of Peter Sutcliffe (complete with stick-on beard that I found convincing, though others did not) and the first credible theory that the tape hoaxer was a serving police officer with a grudge against the man leading the Ripper Squad. The series debuted well and contained new and important information. This was the standard I wanted *Real Crime* to maintain.

The three most successful programmes for ratings in the first series told me something I had not fully appreciated about crime on television. All had a strong female element. Crime had traditionally been seen as a male domain – *The Sweeney*, *The Bill*, *Starsky and Hutch*, *Inspector Morse*, *A Touch of Frost*. But it was interesting to see how the audience grew and the appeal widened for dramas such as *Prime Suspect*, starring Helen Mirren, and *Juliet Bravo*, starring Anna Carteret.

'Ben Needham: Somebody Knows', produced by Richard Belfield of Fulcrum TV; 'The Rachel Nickell Case', produced by Geoffrey Seed and Jonathan Dent for Carlton TV; and 'Who Killed the Pageant Queen? The JonBenet Ramsey Case', produced by David Mills, all included this most crucial aspect – crime stories with a strong female angle. The Ben Needham case was every mother's nightmare – a toddler vanishes on a Greek holiday island and isn't seen for 10 years; Rachel Nickell, the blonde and beautiful mother killed on Wimbledon Common in front of her infant son – her striking image forever captured on video, fooling around in the same park weeks before her death; JonBenet Ramsey, the six year-old US beauty princess bludgeoned in her own home on Christmas Day evening. We demonstrated so many flaws in the police case that the District Attorney stripped them of the investigation. It was watched by 40 per cent of the television audience between at 10.30pm on Wednesday, July 11, 2001, with six million viewers still glued to the set as the credits rolled at 11.30pm.

The *Real Crime* stories featured in this book are showcase examples of bringing new information to well-known cases. 'The Heiress and the Kidnapper' is the remarkable story of the kidnap and murder of Lesley Whittle; remarkable for the honesty with which the investigating officer admits to how the police search faltered and failed. 'Jeremy Bamber' is the tale of a family tragedy. How an adopted son killed his entire family – mother, father, beautiful sister and her two children – and tried desperately but ultimately unsuccessfully, to plead his innocence. 'Kenneth Noye: A Face from the Past' reveals how a 19 year old girl, Danielle Cable, braved the wrath of Britain's most wanted murderer, going undercover in a Spanish bar to identify him to the police. 'Girlsnatcher' is the story of Leanne Tiernan, who went missing from her home in Leeds. Leanne was 16, and dearly loved by family and friends. For three months her mother left the kitchen door unlocked, hoping Leanne would sneak back home. 'I kept thinking that she might have lost her key or forgotten which one was for the back door,' she recalls. Such poignancy is laced through each of our tales; the fears, hopes and cares of close friends, starkly contrasting with awful, brutal acts of violence.

Is there too much crime on TV? Do producers exploit the macabre and horrific for ratings? These are questions with which we wrestle constantly. For every edition of *Real Crime*, producers take great care in the delicate matter of contacting relatives of the deceased to request their assistance. Some brave the camera to talk with great dignity about events most of us can only hope we never have to face. Others, understandably, politely decline but are always kept informed of our intentions. The fact that no-one has ever tried to halt transmission or lodged a complaint is a testament, I would contend, to the sensitivity and thoughtfulness of our production teams.

Meanwhile, millions watch because the most significant crimes fascinate. They tell us something new about the way we live, about subtle movements in society, love and hate, jealousy and revenge. They transform the everyday routine and mundane stuff of life to the dramatic, the unexpected, the shocking. Dickens, in particular, recognised this, so did Shakespeare. In his excellent book: *London – The Biography*, Peter Ackroyd writes of the Cannon Street murder of 1866: 'The murderer was never apprehended, but the characteristics of London mystery are here found in almost emblematic detail – the lodging house in Cannon Street, the heavy rain, the gaslight, the perfectly cleaned shoes. The strange woman shielding herself from the rain only contributes to the air of intimacy and darkness that characterises this crime. Once more it is as if the spirit or atmosphere of the city itself played its part.'

Devotion to detail, understanding the human condition, and dogged determination to establish what really happened are the hallmarks of an important story well told. That is what we have tried to achieve with *Real Crime* on ITV. Just as Edgar Lustgarten did half a century ago.

Steve Anderson
London, June 2003

1 THE HEIRESS AND THE KIDNAPPER

For Detective Chief Superintendent Bob Booth of West Mercia Police, January 14 1975 was just an average working day at Bridgenorth Police Station. At the time, Booth was at the height of his career: he had an impeccable reputation, having solved every one of the 70 murder cases he had investigated; and he had recently been awarded an MBE for his exemplary police work. So, when the police received a call that a young heiress had disappeared from her house overnight, Detective Chief Supt Booth was immediately assigned to the case.

Booth was quickly on the scene, but little did he know how his life would be changed by the case. The kidnap of Lesley Whittle and her subsequent murder would not only reduce Booth's glittering career to tatters, but it would also leave him with deep emotional scars. Despite the 30 years that have passed since that fateful night, Booth is still haunted by the knowledge that several police blunders during the investigation may have cost Lesley her life.

Dorothy Whittle first discovered her daughter's disappearance from the large detached house they shared in the isolated Shropshire village of Highley at around 7 am. It was a cold, unforgiving winter, but Lesley had left the house with only a dressing gown. Hoping her daughter was in the bathroom, Dorothy walked to the bottom of the stairs and called her name. She waited but when there was no reply, she began to suspect that something was dreadfully wrong.

Dashing to check the rest of the property, Dorothy flung each door open to find yet another empty room. Lesley's clothes for the day were still neatly piled on a chair, untouched. Dorothy picked up the telephone to alert her son, Ronald; to Lesley's mysterious disappearance. The line was dead. Panic-stricken and oblivious to the biting January winds, she fled in her flimsy night-clothes to Ronald's house, half a mile away in the village.

She pounded the door with her clenched fists but failed to rouse him. Then she stooped down, grabbed a handful of stones and hurled them at the window until, dazed and bewildered, he peered sleepily through the curtains.

Mother and son frantically searched the small village for the missing teenager but nobody had seen her. Defeated and feeling deeply uneasy, they returned to Mrs Whittle's home, where they were joined by Ronald's heavily pregnant wife, Gaynor.

Ronald immediately telephoned friends and business associates to see if they had any idea of Lesley's whereabouts. While he made the anxious calls, Gaynor spotted a vital clue that strongly suggested Lesley had been taken against her will. Lying in the sitting room hearth was a small section of Dymo tape deposited on a Turkish delight chocolate box with precise instructions for the Whittle family to take £50,000 in a white suitcase to a telephone kiosk in the Swan shopping centre in nearby Kidderminster between 6 pm that night and 1 am the following morning. They were then to await a call for further information. If the police were contacted, Lesley would pay with her life. Despite this warning, however, Ronald's next call was to the police.

Detective Chief Supt Bob Booth's first job was to satisfy himself that the evidence he was presented with was not an elaborate red herring to disguise Lesley's involvement in her own disappearance. 'I quickly built up a picture of Lesley. She wasn't a spoilt child. She appreciated that her mother was paying for her through college and had given her a good education. She was a devoted, responsible child who was deeply loved by her mother. I have never seen a mother so distraught in all my life.'

The police embarked on the arduous task of combing through Lesley's personal belongings. They left no stone unturned. Diaries and address books were all closely scrutinised. Boyfriends and friends were considered as possible suspects.

Booth says: 'She was being educated outside the village at Wolverhampton's Wulfrun College and so she had few friends whom she socialised with locally. She was a hard-working, ambitious girl with dreams of going to university like her boyfriend. She also had a part-time job at a garage in the village to provide her own pocket money. For a girl of that age she was surprisingly mature and was very considerate towards her mother.

'With the profile we had built up, I was perfectly satisfied that she'd been taken from her home against her will. This was no rag day stunt. The girl wasn't pregnant and she hadn't run away with her boyfriend. It was a horribly serious kidnapping and I had to find out what sort of person would do it. Who would be involved in such an awful crime? I never dreamt for a minute that anyone could subject a human being to such incarceration. My first thought was that she was being held hostage in a caravan or a room in a house close to the Whittles' home.'

The stark reality couldn't have been more different. Lesley was screaming for mercy, naked and tethered like a dog in a cold, dark, damp sewer shaft 60 feet below the ground, miles from her comfortable Shropshire home. The kidnapper had led her to her grave.

While Lesley struggled for survival in the bowels of the earth, Booth and his team swung into action, their aim to establish a motive, to trace the kidnapper and, most importantly, to return Lesley to her mother alive.

'Right from the start the safety of the hostage was paramount,' Booth recalls. 'I was focused all the time on her well-being. It was an unusual crime for this country. To my knowledge there had only been one other kidnapping for ransom in this country back in 1970, involving the Hussein Brothers. In that case, the poor lady hostage lost her life, and I vowed that this would not happen this time. I decided that softly, softly, was the approach I should take to get to the bottom of this heinous crime.'

Booth had the benefit of over 25 years' policing experience behind him, but even he was perplexed by the motive and the skilful execution of the kidnap. 'I had to reconcile myself to how a teenager was snatched from her own bedroom in the middle of the night. The family also couldn't comprehend the fact that there was little sign of intrusion. My scene of crime officers told me they had forensic tracings that indicated the path the intruder had taken was to start at the rear of the house and then move up to her bedroom.'

There were no obvious signs of intrusion on any external doors or windows, and it appeared from the forensic evidence that the kidnapper had entered the property through the garage and sneaked his way from there into the main body of the Whittles' home.

What Booth had to determine was why? The Whittle family owned a large transport company in the area, called Whittles Coaches, and had recently been the subject of some high profile publicity surrounding a contested will that somewhat exaggerated the family's wealth. Lesley was due to inherit £82,500 – a significant but not enormous sum in the mid-seventies – from her dead father, and Booth believed that misleading media reports had prompted the kidnap and ransom demands.

Booth had a daughter the same age as Lesley, and in his private moments he found it hard to contain his anger. 'I was really annoyed when I found out about the publicity the family had been subjected to, because it was over-rated. They weren't millionaires. They were responsible business people and had assets, but they were not rolling in money. I don't think Lesley was even aware that she had a legacy awaiting her. She wasn't motivated by money.'

As the hours rolled mercilessly by, the detectives widened their hunt from the family home to the surrounding villages and holiday camps. Police helicopters mounted an aerial search while officers, accompanied by 25 police dogs, combed the area intensively, including hundreds of nearby caravan parks and summer holiday residences in their investigation. But still there was no sign of Lesley.

Privately, Booth could feel the professional detachment his years of duty and training had taught him slipping away and overwhelming emotions threatening to swamp him. 'I was a family man. I had a daughter of Lesley's age living the same kind of life style, so I had this sort of fatherly feeling towards Lesley. Later on I remember thinking, if this is emotional involvement then I've bought it hook, line and sinker.

'I realised early on that this was a genuine ransom demand by people who had forced her, possibly at gunpoint, into the night, naked, apart from her mother's dressing gown. We can only imagine the terror and embarrassment she must have felt.'

Timing was crucial to ensuring Lesley's survival, and Booth was acutely aware that with each hour that passed she was sinking deeper into danger. He was in no doubt that the threat to Lesley's life was serious, and he was eager to convince the abductor that the Whittles had complied with his demands. Booth collected the £50,000 from the Whittles' bank and ensured that every note was microfilmed so that it could be easily traced when the kidnapper eventually spent it. Ronald Whittle agreed to be the courier and because of the death threat he appeared to arrive at the rendezvous unaccompanied.

When Ronald arrived at the meeting place, apparently alone, there were undercover police officers concealed nearby, watching closely, while Inspector Eddie Barry was positioned just 50 yards away in the telephone exchange, poised to record the kidnapper's call when it finally came. There were two telephone kiosks in the Swan Centre shopping precinct and Barry had both covered. He waited and waited, and when the equipment in the exchange indicated that the call was in progress, he eagerly switched on the tape recorder.

But the fateful ransom call to the telephone box was never answered. This was the first in a series of police communication mix-ups, many of which have never been resolved. Barry immediately reported the blunder to Booth.

Booth was furious. The officer he had placed in charge of guiding Ronald Whittle throughout the procedure had aborted the operation without permission when a news leak threatened its success. The police had failed to order a news blackout and, at a critical stage in the investigation, the BBC broke the story in a television bulletin after a local freelance reporter leaked the details to them.

Bob Booth was at the Whittle's home when the story broke. 'I watched the Nine-o'-clock News and just froze,' recalls Booth. 'I thought, well, now the whole world knows about the kidnap and I just hope it doesn't spell the death knell for poor Lesley.'

Booth had decided to continue with the ransom rendezvous regardless, hoping that the kidnapper had missed the evening news and would pursue his plan. His hunch was right. At midnight the kidnapper rang, but because the police officer had aborted the operation there was no one to take the call.

A regional newspaper, *The Birmingham Post*, had also received a tip-off from the same local journalist but had decided not to run with the story. Polly Hepburn, who was the newspaper's young, keen crime reporter at the time, remembers how unlikely the reports seemed.

'We took a phone call at home from a freelance journalist who said he thought a girl had been kidnapped. It seemed so ridiculous and outlandish that we just put the phone down and thought, this just can't be happening.'

After the nine o'clock bulletin on the BBC, Booth recognised that he couldn't keep a lid on the story any longer. In the hope of convincing the kidnapper that Ronald was working on his own to assure the safe return of his sister, Booth held a press conference later that evening.

The story immediately captured the attention of the world's press, even making headlines across the Atlantic in the USA. The tiny rural mining village of Highley was besieged overnight by a media circus hungry for photographs, interviews and the latest updates.

Polly Hepburn, just cutting her teeth on a local paper, suddenly found herself thrust into the midst of one of the most controversial cases in British criminal history. 'I was just starting out covering run-of-the-mill parochial stories and then suddenly there I was, working with the national newspaper guys. Nobody locally had ever covered a story like this. It was pandemonium. It took over the entire village. You have this small community with a little rich girl who goes missing and before you know it the world's press are there.

'It was hard to really get to grips with the fact that a girl of 17, who nobody had ever heard of, could be kidnapped from a small English village. Then to top it all there are ransom notes. It was the stuff of the movies.'

While the press milled ceaselessly around Highley, Lesley's mother, Dorothy Whittle, stayed firmly behind closed doors during the first few weeks of the investigation, trying her best to avoid the persistent media photographers who lurked outside her home hoping to get a picture of the inconsolable mother.

Polly Hepburn caught the occasional glimpse of her. 'She didn't appear at all in the early days. We would sometimes see her at a window and she just looked like a really frail old lady. She must have aged overnight. She must have been dying inside.'

Bob Booth was painfully aware of Dorothy Whittle's grief. 'I have never seen a mother so distressed. A mother losing her child under these circumstances just never gets over it. As the tragedy unfolded she was in constant torment with herself.

'She had no control over Lesley being taken. If she had interfered she would have been killed, without a shadow of a doubt. So it was as well that she slept through the ordeal.'

'She collapsed when details of the kidnapping finally unfolded and when told of Lesley's death it just compounded her grief. In all my years of dealing with bereaved parents, I've learned that no mother can ever really come to terms with her child's disappearance or murder.'

Booth knew instinctively that he was dealing with an organised and complex criminal. 'This wasn't just a momentary attempt to get some money. It was a well-planned, researched crime, and people who do this only target someone after a lot of preparation. I recognised that I was seeking ruthless, merciless, cunning people, and all the time I had to tread warily because there was a death threat hanging over Lesley.'

Despite Booth's determination to catch the kidnapper and return Lesley alive, his efforts seemed to be thwarted at every turn. After the blunder with the missed phone call on the first day of the kidnap Booth decided to send Ronald Whittle back to the telephone kiosk for a second night, desperately hoping that Lesley's abductor would try to make contact again.

He misjudged her captor's intentions and unwittingly steered Lesley's brother into a frenzied paparazzi siege. Photographers crowded around the tiny telephone booth, jamming their lenses against the glass to snatch an exclusive snapshot for the following day's papers.

Ronald had nowhere to hide. Focusing all his attention on the telephone, he willed it to ring, but the call never came. The kidnapper was busy laying a trail of ransom notes in Dudley before delivering his next blow to the Whittle family.

As the case went on, Booth felt that the press were operating with a reprehensible streak that only served to endanger Lesley even further. 'I just can't imagine anything more bizarre in such a serious crime. I'm not against investigative journalism, but there is a limit, and that line has to be drawn when a person's life is at stake. At that time publicity was an obstruction and possibly a liability to ensuring the girl's safety.'

In spite of the publicity and the problems it created, Ronald Whittle retained his composure. It was a virtue that encouraged and impressed Booth. 'Ronald Whittle was dignified and composed throughout. His resilience to this traumatic event was remarkable. He dealt with it with tremendous courage and no outward emotion. Yet I'm sure deep inside his heart must have felt like it had been torn out.' What Booth viewed as an admirable quality in Ronald, however, the media perceived rather differently. Amongst themselves they had firmly placed him in the frame for Lesley's disappearance.

Polly Hepburn had heard the whispers of suspicion amongst the press about the authenticity of Lesley's kidnap. She recalls that it was Ronald's beard that first prompted the media to publicly point the judgemental finger in his direction.

'Ron was very withdrawn and then he grew this little beard that made it look like he was trying to disguise himself. We all wondered why he had grown it. What's worse is that when the Photofits were finally published he looked incredibly like the pictures. It must have been absolutely awful for him because it would be bad enough to go through all that trauma, without people also slyly pointing the finger at you.'

On the third day of the case the kidnapper made his next move. Len Rudd, a family friend who worked as a transport manager for the Whittles, answered a telephone call. The voice on the other end was Lesley's.

In disbelief he pressed the phone closer to his ear. Glancing around the room, he urgently searched for a pen to note down her words. 'Lesley, it's Len. How are you? Where are you?' he spluttered. Lesley's words continued to talk over him. It was a tape recording. Sinking into his seat in utter despair he felt cheated and crushed. He wasn't talking to Lesley. His elation that she was alive and safe was obliterated in seconds.

The tape played twice, allowing Len to record her words accurately. Without delay he passed the message to the police. Lesley was relaying precise instructions for the next stage of the ransom collection. Bob Booth read the message carefully, trying to detect any hidden clues that might indicate the teenager's whereabouts and welfare.

'Hell, I thought. The poor girl! I don't know how she's being treated. I don't know how she's being held. I really feared for her safety.'

Lesley's instructions were clear. 'Mum, you need to go to Kidsgrove Post Office phone box. The instructions are going to be inside. I'm okay, but there are to be no police and no tricks, okay?'

Len had mixed feelings about the taped message. 'At first I was elated. I thought, yes, we've got Lesley back. When I found out it was a pre-recorded tape I just sunk to my shoes. I was gutted.'

His relationship with the Whittles went back a long way. He had known Lesley since she was a baby and had been teaching her to drive in the weeks prior to her abduction.

'When Lesley first went missing all the coach drivers got together and joined the police search for her in all the known places for miles around. We turned this village upside down, but it was hopeless. We couldn't find her.

'She was such a fun, home-loving, happy girl. I would have been proud if she had been my daughter. That is how much I thought of Lesley. She got along with everybody. There was none of that "I'm important and superior and you're just an employee" attitude about her. She behaved like one of us. Nobody had any motive for harming her.

'When I heard the taped phone call she sounded all right. There was no tremor in her voice, no fear. The background had a distinct feeling of vacancy about it. Like she was being held in an empty room. There were no real clues as to her location.'

Detective Chief Supt Bob Booth advised Ronald Whittle to follow Lesley's instructions to the letter and travel to Kidsgrove in Staffordshire, some 75 miles away. To fool the kidnapper into believing that Whittle was acting alone, they fitted him with a radio transmitter, linking him to undercover police officers. Meanwhile, Bob

Booth alerted Staffordshire Police that a highly sensitive ransom run was going to take place in their area.

The diligent security preparations severely delayed the journey, and when Ronald Whittle finally arrived in Kidsgrove he was already over an hour late. Breathless, he pulled open the telephone booth door and anxiously scanned the interior. He picked up the receiver and examined it closely, but there was no sign of any paper attached. He crouched on the floor to look under the ledge, but there was nothing taped there either. Trying to calm himself, he breathed deeply and searched the booth methodically inch by inch.

Finally he spotted something hopeful. He could see a white square protruding from behind the backboard. Easing it out carefully, he confirmed that it was a piece of paper. He unfolded the note and surveyed the scrawled contents. They read: 'Go to the top of the lane and turn into the "No Entry". Go to the wall and flash your lights. Look for torchlight. Run to torch for further instructions placed on the torch.' He glanced at his watch. He'd spent half an hour searching for the message. The next rendezvous was at least a mile away and he was now over an hour and a half late. Would the kidnapper still be there?

Ronald Whittle followed the directions to a nearby Staffordshire beauty spot called Bathpool Park. He turned into the 'No Entry' area as instructed and drove to the end of the lane. Whittle waited, darting his eyes across the deserted land, searching for his signal. Pumped with adrenaline he sat expectantly for an hour, unaware that Lesley was concealed within walking distance. There was no flashing light, and puzzled detectives called a halt to the failed operation unable to understand why the kidnapper had not turned up, despite the fact that, as the instructions had demanded, Ronald had appeared to be completely alone. Lesley's devastated brother went home while the police contemplated their next move.

Booth was at a loss. 'I couldn't see any reason why things shouldn't have gone as planned. Ronald Whittle was there to hand over the money and there were no obvious signs of police backup, so I could only surmise that something had not gone to plan at the kidnapper's end.'

With the benefit of daylight the police surveyed the location. Booth wanted to mount a full-scale search of Bathpool Park. But there was a dilemma. He knew that a high-profile inspection would immediately inform the kidnapper of the police's involvement so he reluctantly compromised and sanctioned a discreet observation by Scotland Yard. Booth felt agitated. He was sure that he was close to solving the kidnap and that Bathpool Park would yield the vital clues.

After several days of mounting anticipation he was stunned when the Yard reported back that they had seen nothing of significance in the park. This momentous oversight delayed the discovery of Lesley and the essential clues that would indisputably link her captor to the crime.

Anxious to maintain contact with the kidnapper and encourage him to proceed with the ransom collection,

Booth persuaded the Whittle family to make a direct appeal through the media.

Ronald Whittle told television reporters: 'I am on the phone at home. I'm there day and night. I'm just hoping they will get in touch with me, but I will make one other point. We have had a number of hoax calls and these people, frankly, are wasting their time. We shall not act, I shall not move from the house, until I have definite proof that Lesley is alive and well.'

Bob Booth had known from day one of the kidnap that he would have to guard carefully against hoaxers. 'When the ransom demands came in I had to discern whether they were genuine. I was fully aware that I could be led up the garden path by some cruel, criminally minded individuals who would jump on the band wagon to make a few thousand pounds, all for the sake of a phone call.'

One such call came in on the second night of the investigation. While Ronald Whittle was patiently waiting at a telephone kiosk for the kidnapper to make contact, detectives intercepted another ransom call in Kidderminster. Orders were given for Mrs Whittle to deliver the £50,000 ransom money to a destination in Gloucestershire. Ronald Whittle was instantly withdrawn from the telephone box and diverted to Gloucestershire under covert police surveillance.

Discretion was vital for the successful execution of the ransom run, so Booth was astounded and furious to hear that a press pack were already on the trail of Ronald Whittle. Officers informed Booth over the radio that hoards of press were following Ronald's car and were in danger of blowing the delicate operation.

Without hesitation, Booth telephoned his head quarters and ordered the information room inspector to close the motorway instantly. Ronald needed time to get ahead of the press and sealing off the motorway was the only way to ensure he would succeed. Shocked by the request, the inspector politely tried to deter Booth. 'You've got no authority to order that, sir.' But Booth was in no mood for resistance: 'Over your dead body, I've got bloody authority to do it now. So close it,' he retorted. The inspector didn't argue and deployed officers to seal off the motorway for ten minutes, giving Ronald the crucial time he needed to make headway.

Ronald periodically glanced in his rear view mirror to check that the surveillance team were still within sight. It was still only day two of the abduction and he hoped that Lesley wouldn't be too traumatised by her ordeal. He even dared to imagine that within hours she could be back home in Highley, safe and well. The nightmare they had all endured over the preceding 48 hours would finally be at an end.

He turned the car off the motorway, diligently following the road signs towards Gloucestershire. Approaching the drop-off point he could see arms and flashlights waving frantically ahead, urging him to stop. As he drew closer, the bleary outlines sharpened into focus.

It was the Gloucestershire Police. They had identified two people lurking near the ransom drop-off point and quickly ascertained that they were ransom hoaxers.

Ronald barely heard the words. Bewildered and angry that the late-night trip had been a wild goose chase, he fought back tears as he thought of Lesley, spending her second night in the clutches of the real kidnapper.

The two hoaxers were subsequently charged and served seven years and four years in prison respectively for their extortion efforts. But there were numerous other hoaxers who made telephone calls during the investigation and slipped through the police net.

Len Rudd was concerned about the effect the hoaxers were having on the family. There were lots of upsets like this for the Whittles. Each time they would have their hopes raised and then cruelly dashed.

'I just don't understand people who ring up and say, "yes, I've seen Lesley" or "I know where she is." Ronald or the police would fly out there to discover that these people weren't trying to help. All they really wanted was a night out on the beer.'

Even the press were duped by the pranks of heartless hoaxers. Polly Hepburn attended an urgent press conference called by the police when they believed they had caught the kidnapper's voice on tape. 'They played this tape and said this is the voice of the kidnapper and somebody out there is shielding him. Please listen to the tape and see if you recognise the voice. It could be your boyfriend, husband or father.'

It transpired that the voice was that of a hoaxer. The real abductor was too cunning to leave a voice recording, instead preferring to use Lesley Whittle to record messages, or to punch them out on a Dymo tape gun.

There were also well-meaning members of the public who inadvertently misled the police. Calls flooded into the information room from people who had spotted someone they truly believed fitted Lesley's description. Booth could take no chances and had to follow every possible lead. 'We went all over the place chasing up information that Lesley had booked into a hotel with a man or been seen in a taxi. None of them were Lesley, just girls who looked like her.'

A broken Dorothy Whittle finally decided to break her silence and appeal to the kidnapper to release her daughter. When a television reporter asked her if she would soon fear the worst, Dorothy replied. 'I suppose I must. I don't know. You know, I don't get round to thinking that way. If we could just know something. If somebody would just contact us. Anyhow. We don't care how.'

But the appeal was too late. The kidnapper wasn't going to make contact, as a dramatic new development was about to reveal.

West Midlands Police invited Bob Booth to examine a stolen car, which had been abandoned in Dudley on the second night of the kidnap. Just 300 yards from where the Connaught Green Morris 1300 was discovered, a gunman had opened fire on security guard Gerald Smith outside the Freightliners railway depot. Smith had spotted a tramp acting suspiciously and confronted him.

The 'tramp' mowed him down in a hail of bullets and fled, leaving the security officer fighting for his life. West Midlands Police sealed off the scene of the shooting for forensic examination, but they didn't notice the abandoned car until eight days later. When they did, they discovered several suspicious items that they believed linked the driver to the disappearance of Lesley Whittle. The delay was another police blunder that cost Booth valuable time in his investigation and may have cost Lesley her life.

When he arrived at the scene in Dudley, Booth was handed a cassette tape taken from the car. 'I hoped and prayed that the cassette was going to play music. What I didn't want to hear was the voice of Lesley Whittle. I had this gut feeling that if it was her voice on the tape then we were doomed.'

Trembling he placed the tape in the cassette player and pressed play. Lesley's voice broke the silence.

'Mum, go onto the M6 north to junction 10 ... and onto the A454 towards Walsall. Instructions are taped under the shelf of a telephone box. There is no need to worry, mum. I'm okay. I got a bit wet, but I am quite dry now. I'm being treated very well. Okay?'

The significance of the tape, the discovery of the stolen car and the description of the gunman who shot Gerald Smith six times in cold blood filled Booth with anxiety. He realised that he was probably in possession of the car used to kidnap Lesley Whittle and that her abductor had firearms and wasn't afraid to use them.

The car yielded other clues. The kidnapper had crudely drawn details of a ransom run on four envelopes, involving telephone boxes all over the Midlands.

The trail followed a route Ronald Whittle would have taken if he hadn't missed the crucial call at the Swan

Centre on the first night of the kidnap. The directions led to two kiosks in Dudley, just yards from where the kidnapper's car had been abandoned.

The instructions directed Ronald Whittle to drive across the bridge towards the Freightliners depot, the location where Gerald Smith was shot. On a nearby lamp-post, police found another crucial piece of Dymo tape. It said, 'Cross road onto car park to gate eight of Dudley Zoo.' The gate was directly in line with where Gerald Smith was shot.

Closer examination of gate eight produced another piece of Dymo tape. The message gave instructions to tie the suitcase to the end of the rope. Police found some rope nearby, and Booth deduced that the kidnapper had planned to use it to drag the ransom money over the wall into the grounds of Dudley Zoo and then make his escape through the caves. 'It was a well conceived plan. He would have been able to escape any surveillance we would have had in place on the car park outside.'

Booth realised that while Ronald Whittle was waiting in a telephone kiosk hoping for a call on the second night of the abduction, the kidnapper was laying ransom notes to a drop-off point at Dudley Zoo. His behaviour had aroused the suspicion of the security guard, and when he moved closer to investigate, the tramp-like figure had blasted him out of the way.

Worse revelations were still to come. Scientific tests of several bullets recovered from Gerald Smith's punctured body were an identical match to others used in murders by Britain's most wanted man. Bob Booth swallowed hard. Lesley Whittle was in the hands of the infamous Black Panther.

'I was dealing with a most ruthless, merciless killer, and there was no doubt in my mind at all that, at the drop of a hat, he would kill again.'

The Black Panther had embarked on his reign of terror a year earlier. Police believed he was the hooded gunman responsible for murdering sub-postmaster Donald Skepper in Harrogate, North Yorkshire.

At the time, Det Chief Supt Bill Dolby of North Yorkshire Police who led the case recognised the remorseless brutality of the Black Panther. He told a news conference: 'My impression of this man is a man who is quite cold, utterly ruthless if he meets the slightest opposition at all. He is a man with no compunction about taking human life. Any member of the public who has any thoughts at all about having a go with this man, my advice to them is: don't. I repeat: don't.'

Police linked the Black Panter to dozens of unsolved robberies in which the intruder had used a brace-and-bit to force open windows, had slashed telephone wires and always worn a black hood to protect his identity.

Lancashire Police were also on his trail. They suspected the Black Panther of killing another man, Derek Astin, during a late-night confrontation in Accrington. Det Chief Supt Joe Mounsey of Lancashire Police summed the Black Panther up as, 'A man who is obviously a thinker. He's cold and I think one can say that he's obviously ruthless. And the worry is, of course, that he may do it again.'

He did strike again. Within two months he shot dead postmaster Sidney Grayland and viciously battered his defenceless wife, Peggy, with a pistol. He escaped from their post office in Langley, West Midlands, with £800 in cash and postal orders. The Black Panther had killed three times in nine months when he set his ruthless sights on 17-year-old Lesley Whittle.

Booth knew he had to act quickly if he had any chance of finding Lesley alive. 'Once I'd linked the Whittle investigation to the shooting at Dudley I asked for all traffic wardens and fixed penalty notices to be checked over a period before and after the theft of the kidnap vehicle.'

A traffic warden came forward who had a notebook filed at the divisional HQ containing details of the kidnap vehicle. His notes led Booth to surmise that the Black Panther had stolen the car the previous October, used it in November during the murder and robbery of Sidney Grayland, and then used it again to deposit stolen money into banks in the Redditch area. The car had also probably been used to abduct Lesley Whittle from Highley, and its final journey was to lay the ransom trail in Dudley.

Other witnesses came forward offering descriptions of a man they had seen with the vehicle. The police were beginning to build up a picture of their suspect. They were looking for an agile 30 to 35-year-old male, who carried firearms, was prepared to adopt disguises and fake regional accents, and usually wore a hood.

Booth says, 'He had spared nobody. I knew that he had shot people with a .22 pistol at point blank range in their bed when they had moved slightly under the bed-clothes.

'Sidney Grayland had suffered for four years as a prisoner of war at the hands of the Japanese, and having survived all that he was then senselessly gunned down by the Black Panther.

'Not content with killing Sidney, the Panther then walked into the post office and brutally battered the postmaster's wife, Peggy, so hard that the police officer who found her didn't even recognise her. She was covered in blood and left for dead. She had a cord bound tightly around her wrist where she had been tied up and dragged across the floor before being battered to a pulp.'

By now more than 600 detectives across several forces were working on the kidnap case and Booth was running a multi-million-pound operation, solely to hunt down and arrest one ruthless killer.

Booth surmised that the Black Panther was fully aware of counter surveillance methods and was so methodical he was unlikely to leave much forensic evidence at the scenes of his crimes.

'The pressure kept building. It was absolute organised chaos, with phones ringing constantly and people coming forward with conflicting information. In no time at all we had about 2,000 actions to clear suspects. And during all this time I was still trying to find a girl who was in jeopardy and return her home.'

Booth knew he couldn't delay telling the Whittles any longer. He would have to break the news that they suspected Lesley was being held captive by the Black

Panther before they read it in the newspapers. 'It was as much as they could bear. I know Mrs Whittle collapsed more than once, and Ronald took the news as best he could, but inside I'm sure he felt completely shattered by it.'

As the manhunt continued nationwide, the world's press lapped up every last detail of the sinister story that seemed to take on a bizarre new twist each day.

It wasn't just the police who received anonymous calls and intelligence about the kidnap. Polly Hepburn had received a tip-off that Lesley was in the hands of the Black Panther days before the police released official details to the media. She decided to confront Bob Booth with the information before making it public. 'I arranged to speak to Bob in the control room to check the accuracy of the tip-off. He categorically denied it, telling me that the Black Panther wasn't in the frame. He said the investigation was not going down that road and made it perfectly clear I was going to look very silly if I went with it.'

Three days later a senior police officer gave Polly the same tip-off. 'Polly, take it from me, this is a real scoop. It will be big news,' the officer assured her.

But Polly wasn't convinced. 'Look, I've already checked this lead with Bob Booth and he told me there was no truth in it whatsoever. He warned me that I could look very foolish if I persisted with the story,' she explained. But the police officer was insistent and asserted that the link with the Black Panther would be announced officially later that evening. 'It's up to you, Polly, but believe me, what I'm telling you now will be announced to the world's press later today. Here's your chance to reveal it first. Don't say I didn't warn you.' Confused about why Bob Booth would blatantly mislead her, Polly rang her editor and explained her dilemma. *The Birmingham Post* decided to take a chance and ran with the story in their next edition.

At 10.30 pm Bob Booth called a press conference at Dudley police station and, as the officer who spoke to Polly Hepburn had predicted, Booth confirmed that the police had incontrovertible evidence that Lesley was in the hands of the Black Panther. Polly arrived late at the conference only catching the tail end of the statement. Psyched up, she was swept along by the electric atmosphere surging through the conference room, but bristling with anger that Bob Booth had deliberately misled her.

'I was incredibly angry. Luckily *The Birmingham Post* was able to run with the story first because the nationals missed their Midland edition deadlines. So it still looked like we were ahead of the rest. I can understand him wanting to keep a lid on it, but once he realised I had the story he shouldn't have denied it. We were the local paper and there's no reason why we shouldn't run with the news first, if we had it.

'I don't know why Detective Chief Supt Booth misled me. I think maybe the police were out of their depth. It was a sleepy rural backwater where not much happened and suddenly they were confronted with a high profile kidnap. At first, I'm sure they thought, as we did, that it would turn out to be a domestic with a boyfriend or something like that, but it turned out to be something far more sinister than any of us could conceive.

'It would have been better for everybody if they had ordered a news blackout but still kept the press informed. They certainly shouldn't have had Ron Whittle, news reporters and police officers careering around like they were in the early days of the investigation.'

The kidnap case was gathering momentum in the media. Polly was working around the clock trying to ensure she delivered up-to-the-minute information. 'It was just the biggest news story ever. It was big enough that a local heiress had been kidnapped, but then to get down the line and find that a man that the police were hunting called the Black Panther could be the same guy ... Well, it just seemed beyond belief.'

Terror gripped the public, and for the first time the panic was beginning to penetrate the seemingly resilient press pack. Polly Hepburn noticed a gradual change in the mood of both the media and the news-hungry public, who so far couldn't get enough of the story. 'For the first time people were genuinely scared. Once we had got over the initial shock that the Black Panther was involved, reality set in and we were wondering where he would strike next. It was especially terrifying for the people running sub-post offices in tiny villages because they were the most likely targets.'

Bob Booth was becoming increasingly nervous too. The kidnapper had ceased contact and the trail had gone cold.

But for Bob there was one lead that had yet to be fully

explored. He says, 'I had this nagging doubt that something was waiting to be discovered at Bathpool Park. I was mulling over how I could search it thoroughly without being in breach of the ransom instructions not to involve the police.' For once, Booth's prayers were answered. A stranger approached him while he was grabbing a late-night snack at a hotel. The man introduced himself as Tom Mangold, a reporter working for the BBC. Mangold offered his professional services to the investigation. It was just the opportunity Booth had been looking for. 'I thought, this is heaven sent and I'm going to capitalise on it.' Booth devised a plan.

Booth agreed to take part in a programme called *Midweek* to talk about the kidnapping. He revealed his motives to Ronald Whittle and instructed him to mention in the televised interview that he had been to Bathpool Park to answer a ransom demand. When the reporter questioned Booth about the ransom run, he feigned concerned surprise and pretended he knew nothing about Whittle's contact with the kidnapper.

In the interview Tom Mangold asked Booth: 'Are you going to have to go for this man if he contacts Ronnie Whittle again?'

Booth: Pardon? 'Again?' What do you mean 'again?'

Mangold: Whittle says he's already made a contact. I would have thought you would have known about this.

Booth: But I don't know about it, until you've raised it just now. How did you get to know about it?

Mangold: Well, we spoke to Whittle yesterday, and he said it was the first time he had mentioned it to the press, and I wasn't quite clear whether he'd mentioned it to you.

Booth: Are you telling me now that Ronald Whittle has been out somewhere, dealing with a man he believes to be the kidnapper? Is that what you're saying?

Mangold: Well, I'm simply saying that that's what Ronnie Whittle told me.

Booth: Well then, I'm afraid that this interview has got to terminate.

'When I first told Tom Mangold what I was planning to do, he said, "That's a bit strong." I said, "It's more than strong. It's a deception but it is intended to persuade the kidnapper that the police are not involved." '

The programme-makers and the other police forces involved in the case were briefed about the planned red herring. But if the kidnapper was duped by the ploy, the press certainly weren't taken in.

Polly Hepburn was confused by the interview. 'I don't suppose the rest of the world watching suspected anything, but for us, the media, we wondered what was going on. It was clear to us that it was a complete setup. It was so unnatural and staged. We just couldn't work out what was happening.'

Booth, however, firmly believed that the kidnapper would be convinced by the interview and would understand that the police now had a legitimate reason to search Bathpool Park. 'I was fully aware that it was an awful deception, but it was an operational means of getting through to the kidnapper,' Booth says.

'The publicity surrounding the case was phenomenal. It was the scoop of the year for the press, and yet still we had had no sightings of any vehicle at the kidnap point, no sightings at the house of any person responsible. So I thought, I'm going to turn the tables. I'm going to use the media in every shape and form to put pressure on the kidnapper to bring this girl back alive. It was my only weapon.'

He knew deep down that it was becoming increasingly unlikely that he would find Lesley alive if he didn't identify the hostage location soon. 'I was acutely aware that in Latin and Continental countries people are kept hostage for months against extortionate ransom demands, but I didn't think the same applied in this country. In my heart I was convinced Lesley was living on borrowed time.'

The fresh search at Bathpool Park began, seven weeks after Lesley's disappearance and Scotland Yard's initial observation of the area. Booth's worst fears were realised. Several vital clues were discovered in the search. Significant clues that had been missed by Scotland Yard and, worse still, had disastrously delayed Booth's painstaking investigation.

Police officers discovered another piece of Dymo tape discarded by a land drain, which read: 'Drop suitcase into hole.' Further examination of the park uncovered a torch, on which the Dymo tape message had previously been fixed, and a spanner that had been used to unlock metal grill bars on a nearby drain.

Booth felt sick. 'I just couldn't believe it. My trust had

gone into the Yard telling me that there was nothing of significance there, and here I was confronted with evidence I never thought to hear about in my wildest dreams. You didn't even have to search for it. It was just there for you to see when you walked through the park.'

Scene of crime officer Detective Constable Philip Maskery was called in to follow the trail of clues that led to a network of underground shafts that ran beneath the park. Apprehensively he made his way to the land drain that had been earmarked as a drop-off point for the ransom. His eyes travelled slowly across the scene. The ground was stark and bare. The first shoots of vegetation were fighting their way through the winter frosts, but there was little of beauty at Bathpool Park at this time of year.

Maskery fixed a rope around his waist and was lowered carefully into the shaft. Working his way through the debris that had been hurled down by local children, he discovered the first two items of significance. Lying amongst the discarded refuse at the base of the shaft was a Dymo tape gun and a roll of Elastoplast. Maskery retrieved both, aware that the tape gun could have been used by the kidnapper to leave messages, but unsure about the relevance of the Elastoplast. The ominous role of the plaster tape was soon to become apparent.

Adjusting his eyes to the darkness and with only a small hand torch for guidance, Maskery noticed a cramped underground passage leading towards the main shaft. Assessing it quickly, he judged that it was unsafe to crawl along the passage and steadily made his way back to the surface to discuss his findings with the rest of the team.

'I was chilled to think I might have been in the area where the kidnapper had operated, but at that point I wasn't prepared for what we were going to discover next,' he says.

The team turned their attention to a raised area of the park, adjacent to another shaft directly in line with the one Philip Maskery had inspected. Recently, local children had stumbled across a discarded pair of Zeiss binoculars and a leather jacket at the scene and handed the items in to the police.

Maskery immediately spotted that the bolt on the manhole cover had been loosened. A wave of nauseous anticipation swept over him as his mind wrestled with images of what might lurk in the cramped cavity below.

But before he could descend the 60-foot-deep shaft, the team had to rule out the possibility of deadly methane gas stirring silently beneath them in the tunnels of the disused Nelson's coal mine. Maskery stood patiently, the minutes slowly ticking by as he waited for the green light to proceed with his onerous mission.

The local council tested the labyrinth of tunnels and, as suspected, they proved positive for methane. The shaft entrances around the area were opened, and the team of police officers could feel the air begin to change around them. The men looked nervously at each other. It felt like an omen. Later that day the council officials tested the tunnels again and this time they declared it was safe for Maskery to enter.

Treading warily, he approached the shaft entrance. Wearing only soft rubber-soled Wellingtons, he lowered himself gradually into the drain. Sinking deeper, he was enveloped by the echoing darkness and stale, clammy air clung to his damp skin.

Halfway down, something caught his eye. He flashed his torchlight over the obscure outline he could just make out in the dim beam. Quickly scanning an array of objects, he mentally noted a tape recorder, batteries, pens and a reporter's notepad.

Glancing down, he spotted something crudely wrapped up in a plastic bag. Expectantly, Maskery descended further towards the package. He pulled the plastic wrapping apart tentatively and peered inside. With relief he realised it was a sleeping bag inside, not a body, so he continued his search, venturing deeper into the inhospitable labyrinth of tunnels. Sudden noises pierced the chilling stillness – scurrying sounds and cascading water which raced through the arterial drains threatening to drench and overpower any obstacle in its path. In the distance he could hear the echo of trains whistling through the Harecastle tunnel up above.

Trying to blot out the menacing noises, he pressed on with his search. 'On the bottom level beneath the sleeping bag I noticed a piece of foam. To the side there was a garment hung on a girder.' He moved towards the limp material, prising it apart to identify it. It was a dressing gown. Probably the same dressing gown that Lesley Whittle had disappeared in several weeks earlier. Placing it back on the girder he turned slowly. The area was cramped and there was little room for manoeuvre. His eyes followed the trail of a thin, twisting section of wire hose glinting in the tiny beam of his flashlight. The metal wire was bolted securely to a footstep carved out of the crumbling concrete. It travelled across the foam and the sleeping bag and disappeared without trace underneath.

Crawling forwards, Maskery peered over the ledge to follow the trail. Careful to keep his balance, he inched his head hesitantly over the platform, glancing down and then jumping back instantly. He was face to face with Lesley Whittle.

The naked teenager was hanging, strangled by a crude noose fashioned out of the other end of the wire hose. The only glimmer of compassion shown by her captor was a section of Elastoplast bound around the noose to cushion her flesh as the wire cut into her skin. Defenceless, Lesley had been tethered like a dog throughout her isolated and harsh confinement.

'There was this 17-year-old girl, tied up at the bottom of this cold, dark, shaft with no clothes on. To think that a man is capable of kidnapping a girl and bringing her to an environment like that to die is beyond words. It was a very lonely place. That horrific scene has gone through my mind many, many times' recalls Maskery.

Paralysed by shock, Maskery struggled to gather his thoughts and continue with his job. On the ledge below Lesley he retrieved some three-inch-wide strips of used Elastoplast. One of them had some of Lesley's eyebrows attached to it and had been used as a blindfold. Maskery recoiled in horror. He knew that photographs would have to be taken before the body could be moved, so, without looking back, he made his way carefully through the shaft to inform his colleagues above ground.

It seemed to take so much longer to climb to the shaft entrance than it had to lower himself into Lesley's grave.

And when he finally emerged, Maskery was very aware of the press gathered nearby, who were observing every move with telephoto lenses. 'I think they could see from the expression on my face that I had discovered something significant and they tried to get closer to us to find out more.'

While Staffordshire police mobilised to do a forensic search of the remainder of the shaft, and photograph and remove the body, Bob Booth had the unenviable task of informing Lesley's family that she was dead.

Booth knew there was no time to spare if he was to reach the Whittles with the grim revelation before the media approached them for a comment. Filled with trepidation, he picked up the telephone and dialled Ronald Whittle's number. It was the call he had prayed so hard that he would never have to make.

'I said, "I hate doing this over the telephone, Ronald, but I think your sister has been found. She is dead in a shaft at Bathpool Park." I'm sure he broke down at that point. I was close to it. I was totally demoralised. I felt so much had hampered the progress of my investigation, such as the kidnap vehicle and Bathpool Park not being searched in time. If only we'd found these things earlier we could have saved the Whittles all that terrible anguish. The family paid for it dearly and Gaynor,

Ronald's wife, lost her baby, probably as a result of the insurmountable stress.'

The Whittle family's vigil of hope and prayers was at an end. Their worst nightmare had been realised. Things couldn't get any worse. But for Bob Booth, the nightmare was far from over.

A careless choice of words brought him a new headache. 'I was certainly at risk of being accused of negligence because Lesley Whittle had lost her life. I knew Fleet Street were baying for my blood regarding these apparent failures and then I compounded it. I made a remark that, although Staffordshire Police had our body, we would continue with our investigation and that we would have an arrest in 24 hours. What I failed to say was, "If that was humanly possible."

'It sparked a series of headlines promising an arrest in 24 hours, which, of course, I knew was impossible. People once again started to assume the possible involvement of Ronald Whittle, because they couldn't conceive any other way of achieving an arrest unless someone was already in the frame. To some cynical members of the press and public he seemed the obvious suspect. I deeply regretted that choice of words because it created yet more unnecessary heartache for both Ronald and myself.'

Polly Hepburn remembers the strange anti-climax amongst the media once Lesley's body was discovered. 'It was all a bit cold and clinical because we knew before we went to the press conference that the body must be Lesley's. There was this strange sort of eerie quiet. A sort of, so this is it, she is dead. I don't think at that stage we knew she was naked, or realised the full extent of the horror of her hostage place until the court case. It was very quiet and sad and we just sat there thinking, right, well, where do we go from here?'

As the details of Lesley's confinement became apparent, Booth slipped further into despair. 'Lesley had been tethered with a wire looped around her neck. It was fastened so securely with U-bolt grips that she would never have been able to release them. We found out in subsequent enquiries that Lesley did scream for help. But, sadly, her distant screams were dismissed as the sounds of children playing by several people who heard them in the park, so, regrettably, those screams were never heeded. 'I think she must have been absolutely terrified. Anyone would be, man or woman, let alone a teenager. To think that she could hear people walking above and she screamed with all her might for help and mercy and nobody came to her rescue … It must have been a horrifying ordeal.' Lesley's only contact with the living world was the vermin and insects crawling over her flesh.

The funeral provided a fresh batch of headlines for the media and another heartrending endurance test for the grief-stricken and weary Whittle family.

Polly Hepburn attended the funeral on behalf of *The Birmingham Post*. 'It was surreal. It was held at a tiny village church in Highley, Shropshire, and because it had been snowing heavily in the days before, it looked like a Christmas card setting. The church was absolutely packed with people. Not just family and friends, but public mourners who came to watch, the police and, of course, the photographers and press. I remember seeing Mrs Whittle in the funeral cortege and she looked completely bewildered. She didn't make eye contact with anyone and had clearly been weeping. She reached into her bag for a pair of sunglasses to cover her reddened eyes. I think the funeral was just the final proof for her that it was all over for her daughter.'

Detective Bob Booth snaked his way through the crowds to pay his last respects to Lesley and privately make his peace with her for failing to find her alive. 'There aren't many funerals of victims I have attended, but I felt I had to go to this one to demonstrate my gratitude to the Whittles for the trust they placed in me. I felt such deep sorrow for them.'

With the funeral behind him, Detective Chief Supt Bob Booth still had the unenviable task of capturing the kidnapper and trying to work out why the ransom collection had failed and therefore resulted so tragically in Lesley Whittle's death.

His inquiries unearthed some disturbing evidence. 'It was some time after the inquest that I found out that two witnesses had been at Bathpool Park on the same night as Ronald Whittle's failed ransom operation.'

Staffordshire nightclub disc jockey Peter Shorto and his girlfriend arrived at the beauty spot, a regular haunt of courting couples, at 2.45 in the morning. Fifteen minutes later they were disturbed by a torch light flashing on and off several yards in front of their vehicle. 'Don't worry,' Peter reassured his girlfriend, 'it's probably just someone out walking their dog.' Another beam of light panned across the car park. It was headlights. As the vehicle parked up nearby Peter noticed the interior light being switched on and one of the occupants lighting a cigarette. 'It's just a policeman stopping for a smoke, nothing to worry about,' he reiterated.

A quarter of an hour later the couple were alarmed again, this time by a van that pulled up abruptly in front of them and flashed its headlights on and off before speeding away. Peter turned to his girlfriend: 'Not much point sticking around here tonight. There's too much activity. Let's go.' They left the park and didn't give any more thought to the strange series of incidents until details of the failed ransom run were revealed. Then, realising that they might have been unwittingly at the centre of the failed operation, they contacted the police to make a statement.

This new evidence threw fresh light on the case for Booth. 'I read the statement and it took me back a bit. I concluded that the kidnapper must have thought that Peter Shorto's car was Ronald Whittle's vehicle and, on seeing a police car turn up, he panicked and fled.

'That panic is clearly illustrated by him spilling several articles, such as the notepad and pens, from his holdall as he tried to remove evidence from the shaft. He thought the police were closing in on him and had to erase his tracks before he could make a getaway.

'It was the most devastating death for Lesley because in the process she was strangled by being pushed over the ledge by the killer.

'I've always believed he did this intentionally because he was angry about the police intrusion and because in his panic he had forgotten to put his hood on and she had seen him and would be able to identify him.

'The Black Panther had made it quite clear in his ransom messages that there was to be no police or tricks because Lesley would pay the price with her death. And here we have a police car rolling up at the moment he is expecting her ransom money to be handed over. In my opinion, he vented his anger by pushing her to her death down that hell-hole of a place. I firmly believe it was murder.'

It seemed that on the very night that Ronald Whittle was pinning all his hopes on bringing his sister back alive, an inadvertent police presence may, in fact, have triggered a series of events leading to her death.

But Staffordshire Police strongly disputed Peter Shorto's claim that one of their police cars had been in the vicinity that night. Detective Chief Supt Harold Wright launched an internal inquiry for Staffordshire Police and concluded: 'We've got to accept that there was a courting couple in Bathpool Park that night. We've got to accept they saw a police vehicle, or something that to them resembled a police vehicle. They did not see a Staffordshire police vehicle, because there was no Staffordshire officer or vehicle near Bathpool Park that night.'

The presence of the police car remains a mystery, but the dispute caused a deep rift between Detective Chief Supt Booth and his fellow officers. His insistence that a

Staffordshire police car had driven into the park, panicked the kidnapper and compromised the ransom run brought accusations of disloyalty from his peers. His superiors increasingly perceived him as a loose cannon and, anxious to avoid further embarrassment and conflict, they minimised his further involvement in the Lesley Whittle case.

Scotland Yard appointed their top man, head of their International Murder Squad, Commander John Morrison, to lead the investigation, alongside Inspector Wally Boreham, who was put in charge of the incident room.

Booth regarded this as another police move that was detrimental to the investigation. 'Scotland Yard was just a figurehead. They didn't bring any expertise with them that wasn't already in place. The local detective chief superintendent has the loyalty of his men, he has local knowledge and the support of people in the locality, and bringing in outsiders was not beneficial to the investigation.'

Booth tried to rub along with his new colleagues but felt compromised by their intentions. 'Morrison didn't want the role of the Scotland Yard surveillance team revealed. I told him I had kept it quiet so far but that when I was called to give evidence in court that was where my loyalty to Scotland Yard ceased. It didn't go down very well and did nothing to ingratiate me with my new colleagues.'

Scotland Yard and Staffordshire Police complained to Booth's superiors that he was hindering the investigation by not co-operating with them. Their grievance was acknowledged and Bob Booth was sent back to Bridgnorth station and humiliatingly sidelined in the case.

Staffordshire Police and Scotland Yard took charge of the investigation. Detective Inspector Wally Boreham surveyed the evidence before him. 'In this case it was almost unique. We were inundated with clues. There was the mattress, there were the Zeiss binoculars that were found in the park, there was the Dymo tape, a tape recorder found in the shaft where Lesley died, and so it went on. We were absolutely inundated. We had an embarrassment of riches for clues.'

Detectives began tracing where the abandoned items had been purchased, confident that the paper trail would lead them to the kidnapper.

Detective Chief Supt Booth had also previously issued officers with an information card detailing the intelligence that had been gathered so far. 'We had an excellent profile. We even knew the size of [the Black Panther's] footwear and his inside leg measurement. We knew that he used stolen cars and that his preferred transport routes were motorways. These information cards were distributed to remind officers what to look out for during their daily duties.'

To keep the public and press focused on the manhunt the police released a sample of the kidnapper's handwriting, hoping that someone would recognise it. Officers appeared on the television news to demonstrate the kind of wire used as a noose for Lesley, but their greatest hopes were pinned on their most recent find, a fingerprint left on a notepad in the shaft where Lesley was killed. Detectives painstakingly trawled through millions of profiles, but no match was found in the police files. The Black Panther continued to elude them.

Detective Chief Supt Harold Wright was amazed by how the kidnapper repeatedly evaded them. 'We knew everything about the man. We'd got his height, his age, his clothing. We had practically all his personal details except his name and address.'

Britain's biggest manhunt continued for several months after Lesley's body was found, but still there was no sign of a breakthrough. Detectives traced and interviewed nearly 3,000 men who had worked on the transformation of Bathpool Park into a leisure amenity. But the interviews failed to identify a culprit. Then, almost a year after Lesley's disappearance, an unexpected development occurred in Mansfield Woodhouse, Nottinghamshire, over 100 miles from the Whittles' home.

Two police officers had just begun night duty and were sitting in their panda car, hidden from view in a side street. PC Stuart McKenzie was making notes under the streetlight when his colleague, PC Tony White, nudged him and pointed to a man loitering suspiciously near a post office. 'I don't like the look of him. Let's find out what he's doing.' PC McKenzie turned the key in the ignition and they nudged towards the man to take a closer look.

McKenzie pulled up alongside the man and wound down the window. 'My colleague asked him who he was, what was his date of birth and where he was going to. I was writing down the answers, and as we got to the last question I heard a voice say: "Don't move, any tricks and you're dead." I glanced up and was staring down the business end of a double-barrelled shotgun. "Fucking hell!" I shrieked.'

The suspect, who had told them he was a local man called John Moxon, turned to PC White and snapped in guttural tones, 'You, in the back.' Speechless, the officer clambered into the rear of the car and the suspect eased himself into the passenger seat beside McKenzie. Prodding the gun harshly into McKenzie's ribs, he ordered him to drive.

'Half of me was scared out of my mind and the other half was thinking that it was a dream; that it couldn't really be happening. I started to drive, wondering where on earth he was going to take us.'

The car was travelling on the A60 north towards Warsop village. As they ventured further out of Mansfield, the street lighting became less frequent and McKenzie strained to see the road ahead. It was a cold December night and their warm breath began to steam up the windows as they bounced around the cold interior of the car. Tentatively, he wound the window down an inch. Moxon snapped, 'That's enough. Any tricks and you're dead.'

'My mind was racing. I kept thinking, we've got to do something to disarm him or we won't get out of this alive.' Both police officers darted their eyes towards the rear view mirror, trying to communicate without alarming the gunman wedged between them.

Agitated, Moxon sat half-turned in his seat, coiled like a spring and ready to pull the trigger at any sign of betrayal. He spoke only to give further instructions. Eventually, Moxon barked at McKenzie, 'Take me to Blidworth.' They were travelling in the wrong direction and McKenzie knew he would have to turn the car around. He gently asked Moxon for permission and, under his piercing gaze, slowly manoeuvred the vehicle. As he edged around in his seat to get a clearer view of the road, Moxon became suspicious.

'Don't turn around. Don't look at me. Any tricks and you're dead,' he yelled. McKenzie stopped the car and tried to explain that he had to look where he was going or they might have an accident. Moxon fell silent for a minute as if mulling it over and then muttered, 'All right then, but don't look at me.'

As they travelled in silence along the deserted road towards Blidworth, the police radio burst into life. Moxon was startled. He jammed the gun forcefully into the officer's ribs. 'Ignore it. Don't answer them,' he commanded. 'The police will become suspicious if I don't reply,' said McKenzie. 'Let me tell them I'm committed with a motorist and they will leave us alone.'

Moxon reluctantly agreed, but the radio call had made him edgy. He wasn't prepared to take any chances. 'Got any rope? I want to tie you up.'

McKenzie told Moxon no, but keen to appear cooperative, he offered to cut up the seatbelts so that he could tie them up with those. It was getting late and both officers realised that the further they allowed the journey to continue into open countryside, the more their lives were at risk.

In desperation they tried to engage Moxon in conversation. 'Look, we don't want any trouble. We don't want to die. Just tell us what you want. You can have anything.'

McKenzie invented a family, hoping that Moxon would relent rather than leave young children without their father. He pleaded for survival. 'Look, my children want to see me again. We are not going to pull any tricks on you. You can have anything you want, just let us go.' It was hopeless. Moxon wasn't moved by his display of emotion. 'Keep going. Just drive. Any tricks and you're dead,' he spat through clenched teeth.

McKenzie looked up at the mirror, trying to signal to PC White to leap into action while Moxon wasn't looking. 'I believed he was going to kill us. It was racing through my mind the whole time I was driving. I kept thinking that once he got us to Blidworth, which was a small village surrounded by woodland, he would shoot us both and leave us for dead. I realised that he must be a local man because Blidworth was a small place that wasn't well-known and he pronounced it in the local way.'

McKenzie's heart started to pound. He was sure Moxon could hear it. He decided to make a last-ditch attempt at escape – it seemed the only hope for survival. As they approached a fork in the road, he swung the car violently to the right, forcing it over the centre of the road, and then swung it back again, hitting the brakes simultaneously. Moxon and PC White were catapulted from their seats, while McKenzie stabilised himself on the steering wheel. As he brought the vehicle under control, braking abruptly, Moxon fired the gun, tearing a hole in the roof of the car. Mckenzie shot back in his seat, hit the driver's door and rolled out onto the road. As he hit the tarmac White's voice echoed in his ear. 'I've been shot. He's shot me in the hand.' The call for help pulled McKenzie off the ground and he darted to the other side of the vehicle to assist his injured colleague.

'I thought, my God, he has killed him. He's going to be dead.' Flinging the door open he plunged inside the car. 'To my amazement, I saw that despite his injury he'd grabbed Moxon around the neck and was thumping him with his elbow.'

In one swift movement McKenzie dragged the entwined men out of the car, but Moxon was firing on adrenaline and wasn't about to surrender. A local man, Roy Morris, was placing an order at the Junction Chippie fish and chip shop in Rainworth when he heard the commotion outside. Glancing out of the window he saw the two policemen struggling to restrain an assailant and dashed out to help. 'I shouted to the police, "What do you want me to do?" And this officer yells back, "Grab his wrists so that we can handcuff him."

'They were struggling like mad to contain him. His eyes were partially closed and he was shaking with rage. I grabbed his wrists so they could handcuff him and then they dragged him to the railings where they cuffed him again. It all seemed to be over in a flash. Quite a crowd gathered and one man threw a blow at him while he was chained to the railings. In the end the police had to protect him.'

Battered and bruised, John Moxon was taken away for questioning. The holdall he had been carrying was searched. Inside, officers found two watches on one strap, two torches, two sets of batteries, two knives, two razor blades, two pairs of gloves and the legendary Black-Panther-style hood. For two days the suspect refused to speak to anyone. When he finally agreed to talk he reluctantly gave his name. It wasn't John Moxon. He was Donald Neilson, a self-employed joiner from Bradford.

Detectives discovered that he was born Donald Nappey in August 1936. His name had made him the target for bullies both at school and during his National Service. He later changed his name by deed poll to Neilson.

He relished army life and developed an appetite for firearms and survival techniques. He saw action in Cyprus and Aden, and had learned jungle warfare in Kenya. In 1955 he married his fiancée Irene and it was she who persuaded him to turn his back on the army and settle down as a jobbing carpenter in Bradford.

He struggled to make ends meet as a carpenter, and tried and failed to make a success of running a taxi firm and a security guard business. As the financial success he craved continued to elude him, he became domineering towards his wife and child, forcing them to dress up in combat gear and play soldiers.

The police applied to the court for a warrant and mounted a fingertip search of Neilson's home. On first impression it seemed like any other family home, but there was still one room to check, the locked attic in the gable at the top of the house.

As they entered, the officers cast their eyes around the extraordinary assembly of objects exhibited before them. The shabby room was filled with an impressive collection of tools, maps and car keys – all innocuous items until you placed them alongside the black hoods, sawn-off shotgun and ammunition that were stashed in the locked attic as well. The police also found a Dymo labeller with a misplaced letter that matched labels found at Bathpool Park.

One other significant retrieval was a blue balaclava. During one robbery a sub-postmaster had sprayed the intruder with household ammonia, releasing the blue dye from the hat. Forensics compared the dye on the hat with the deposits discovered in the victim's house. It was a perfect match. And, hidden in the back of a drawer, police stumbled across the most revealing evidence of all, a palm-sized model of a Black Panther. After a manhunt lasting almost a year, it seemed that PC McKenzie and PC White had unwittingly come face to face with Britain's most wanted murderer.

The two officers were later awarded the Queen's Gallantry Medal for overpowering the gunman. They were heralded as heroes for years after the incident. PC McKenzie was eventually forced to retire from the force on medical grounds when it was discovered that the tussle with the Black Panther had left him with a perforated eardrum. PC Tony White remained on the force, but in 2001 his glorious reputation was shattered when he was convicted of indecent assault on four teenage girls.

Donald Neilson was transferred to a Staffordshire jail for questioning, where Detective Inspector Wally Boreham struggled to get any sense out of him. 'He would be asked the simplest of questions and he would merely look at the wall and count the bricks for 25 minutes. Then, just as you thought he was not going to answer, he blurted something out. It wasn't necessarily the answer to the question you'd just asked, but he would make some comment. Then you'd follow that up with another question and the same thing would happen again.'

But as police began to reveal the staggering evidence they had acquired, Neilson opted for a different approach. 'He said he would help us. He would tell us all about the murders and make a separate statement for each one.' As the interviews progressed, he confessed to violent robberies at several sub-post offices and to the kidnap of Lesley Whittle, although he insisted that her death was a tragic accident.

Neilson's career in crime dated back to 1965, when he carried out the first of around 400 burglaries. The proceeds were minimal, so Neilson promoted himself and turned to robbing sub-post offices. Between 1967 and 1974 he carried out 19 robberies, but, greedy for higher rewards, he soon upped the ante, embarking on a series of aggravated robberies that resulted in three violent deaths.

He was a single-minded predator and admitted that he had meticulously planned Lesley Whittle's kidnap after reading about her inheritance in a national newspaper. He had spent months researching her background and movements before striking in the dead of night. He was a ruthless, swift, silent killer, and Lesley Whittle stood little chance of survival once she was in his hands.

The police had their man, but he was not quite the character many of them had anticipated. They were surprised to discover that not only was Neilson married but that, shockingly, his daughter, Kathryn, was almost the same age as Lesley Whittle.

Neilson was charged with 13 violent crimes, including four murders. There was a heavy police guard to hold back the thronging crowds outside Oxford Crown Court where he stood trial in July 1976. They were all straining to get a glimpse of the fearsome Black Panther. Some had waited six hours to stake out their position. By the time Neilson arrived, in a convoy of cars, his face hidden from view under a blanket, he was met by over 200 jeering onlookers baying for his blood.

Polly Hepburn recalls: 'There was a huge amount of relief amongst everyone that the police had caught him. After all this time I couldn't wait to see what he looked like. The picture I had built up in my mind based on the police descriptions was of a Territorial Army type. I visualised him as being tall, muscular and a fitness fanatic. In reality he was just this awful little man standing about five foot six and very ordinary looking. I could have passed him in the street a million times and never stopped to think, I wonder if that's the Black Panther.

'I think all the press had assumed he was a Midlands

man, so it was a bit of a shock when we discovered he came from Bradford.' Neilson was a master at faking accents and adopting disguises. When he shot Gerald Smith in Dudley there was no trace of his Bradford accent and Smith firmly believed he was dealing with a local tramp.

The press and jury sat in amazement as the case unfolded in court. Neilson was shown two exhibits, a balaclava and a sawn-off shotgun. Horrified gasps shuddered through the courtroom as he pulled the balaclava over his head, picked up the gun and demonstrated the false voice he had used when he kidnapped Lesley.

'I think for the first time we really got a sense of what it must have been like for Lesley,' recalls Polly. 'He adopted this really strange, guttural staccato voice. It wasn't an accent you could identify. He was barking instructions. Frozen in shock, we all stopped writing. You could see the jury thinking, my God, is this what Lesley Whittle faced? It must have been terrifying beyond belief.'

Seemingly enjoying the notoriety and the opportunity to perform for an audience, Neilson willingly elaborated on each stage of the kidnap. When he was asked to demonstrate to the jury how he had held the chicken wire, Polly remembers him winding it around his hands and sawing at the witness stand with it.

'I couldn't believe what he was doing. I quickly looked around to see whether he could escape if he decided to jump over the witness box. It was really frightening just being there in the same room with him, even though there were lots of other people and police officers standing by. He was on trial but he still seemed to be in control.'

Neilson's defence for every murder was that it was an accident, and Lesley's death was no exception. He told the court he had heard helicopters hovering over Kidsgrove and suspected a police trap. In his panic to gather his belongings and escape he claimed that he had accidentally pushed Lesley to her death.

This contradicted Detective Chief Supt Bob Booth's theory that a police panda car had frightened and angered Neilson, triggering the murder. Prior to the court case Booth had requested a private interview with Neilson. He was keen to meet the man who had cost him his reputation. 'I wanted to find out why we hadn't caught him earlier. He was immediately on the defensive. He was alert and certainly no fool. He assured me he was aware of all methods of surveillance and message relaying, which indicated to me that he had a strong military background.' Neilson said that he had anticipated the intervention of SAS troops by helicopter and a police trap.

Finally face to face with the Black Panther, Booth secretly tape-recorded the interview. The conversation between the two men convinced the detective that he was right about the real reason Lesley was pushed to her death.

There was one section of tape that Booth kept replaying in his head:

Neilson: 'I mean the public loved it, didn't they? I mean it sold papers. If they'd called me the Pink Panther, you wouldn't have got half the response. As I see it we've got two sides. I'm on one side and you're on the other. Somebody is to blame … for that girl's death.

The one thing I want to get at is the bloody truth. What went wrong? I mean, you say you're right. I know for a fact that I'm right. So what went wrong? Tell you what, quite sincerely, I blame you.

Booth: You blame me?

Neilson: Aye.

Booth: Didn't all the public?

Neilson: I'm talking about that lass's death. Do you know I hold you responsible?

Booth: Didn't all the public? Didn't all the public?

Booth interpreted this conversation to mean that Neilson blamed him for sending the police panda car into Bathpool Park and that this resulted in Lesley's death.

'In my view, the arrival of that police car was the one tragic event that was to cause Neilson to kill Lesley. He panicked; he hadn't got his mask on, and because she saw his face she paid for it dearly. It's also possible he was angry at police intervention when he'd made it quite clear that there were to be no tricks, and he vented his fury on that poor girl.

'If I had still been in charge of the investigation and my interview with him had been official, then there is no way I would have let him get away with claiming that Lesley's death was an accident.'

Against the wishes of the police force, Bob Booth went public at the trial with his theory about the events leading up to Lesley's death. He also revealed two more of the investigation's best-kept secrets. He told the jury that Scotland Yard had been involved in the ransom run, and that they had been responsible for the initial disastrous search of Bathpool Park days after Lesley's disappearance.

The trial grabbed headlines around the world for five weeks, but it took the jury just 90 minutes to reach their verdict: guilty of murder. Neilson was given five life sentences and the judge warned him: 'If you are ever released from prison, it should only be on account of great age or infirmity.'

Polly Hepburn believes that Neilson had been caught up in a game of cat and mouse with the police. 'I think he believed he was intellectually superior to the police. It wasn't all about robbing post offices, but became more about beating the police at their own game. I think once he hadn't been caught for the first offence he committed, he grew in confidence and became bolder. He certainly came across during the trial as someone who, despite the circumstances he was in, still felt he was the winner and they were the losers.

'Even in the witness stand I think he enjoyed his 15 minutes of fame. He seemed to get a kick out of being the centre of attention and didn't seem to think he had done anything wrong.'

With Neilson convicted and behind bars, the police turned their attentions to internal affairs. Bob Booth was accused of disloyalty to fellow officers for revealing confidential elements of the operation during the trial and for his continuing insistence that Staffordshire Police were responsible for the failed ransom run at Kidsgrove.

While senior police officers basked in the post-trial media limelight and were feted for their part in the capture and conviction of the Black Panther, Bob Booth was notably absent from all the glory. Disgraced and shunned by his peers and superiors, he was thrown out of the CID and demoted to uniform. This was a man who had solved 70 murders and who had thrown himself wholeheartedly into solving the Whittle case. His glittering career was destroyed in a matter of months.

Decades later, Booth remains tormented, not just by the assassination of his career and professional reputation, but – and probably more so – by his failure to return Lesley home alive.

'We let that girl and the Whittle family down. I have tried to seek the answers but I have been impeded in all my actions to do so and it has lost me a lot of favour in pursuing those avenues. As far as the public were concerned, I was in charge so it was my problem.

'I took the flak. I didn't run around shouting to the public that they should blame the Yard and Staffordshire but not blame me. To do that would have caused anarchy. But when the trial occurred I felt it was time to reveal some of the truth and I paid for that with my career.

'I'm aware that some members of the public may even think to this day that I bear some measure of incompetence in this case. I feel I was a scapegoat. I can only express to Ronald Whittle and his family that all my years of experience were deployed solely with the aim of getting Lesley back alive, that everything was done with her safety in mind and that when things did go wrong it was not of my or my officers' making.'

To Polly Hepburn the reason behind the police mix-ups was evident all along. 'Nobody should point all the blame at the police for the way things turned out, but I think they handled it badly. There was too much inter-fighting going on. If all the police forces had got together and worked out a strategy, then the outcome could have been very different.'

Now retired, Bob Booth no longer has a professional interest in the Neilson case, but he still feels a personal responsibility for safeguarding the public from the infamous Black Panther. 'If he was ever released I don't doubt for a second that he would return to a life of crime. Killers like this should never be allowed to walk the streets again and I will do all in my power to keep him incarcerated.'

Neilson has served over 26 years in prison and recently the Home Secretary informed him that he should expect to spend the rest of his life in prison.

2 JEREMY BAMBER

It was an early August morning in the sleepy Essex village of Tolleshunt D'Arcy. If any residents had been passing White House Farm at that early hour, they would have noticed an unusual sight. Police marksmen were cautiously circling the walls of the Bambers' home while, a little further away from the house, Jeremy Bamber was standing close to Sergeant Douglas Adams, identifying rooms and pointing out where his relations usually slept.

Two hours earlier Jeremy had made a panic-stricken call to Chelmsford Police Station, some 15 miles away, reporting that his family were in grave danger. It was August 7 1985.

Bamber informed the duty officer that his adoptive father, Nevill Bamber, had telephoned him pleading for help because Jeremy's sister, Sheila, had 'gone crazy' and was armed with a gun. He told the officer that, as Nevill was mid-sentence, the line went dead. As if someone had terminated the call.

Jeremy explained that he had tried to alert the local station at Witham but there was no reply, so he called Chelmsford Police instead. PC Michael West immediately contacted Witham Station by radio and reassured Jeremy that a police car was on its way. At PC West's request Bamber set off to White House Farm to liaise with the police officers there.

When he arrived, Jeremy Bamber was met by three officers: Sergeant Christopher Bews, PC Robin Saxby and PC Stephen Myall. Bamber told the officers that his parents, Nevill and June Bamber, his sister, Sheila, and her twin sons were inside the house. He scribbled a list of the firearms stocked in the gun cupboard and handed it to the officers.

PC Myall asked whether Sheila would be more annoyed at seeing Jeremy or the police. Jeremy admitted that Sheila didn't like him but thought she would be equally unhappy to see the police. The main consideration at this stage was whether Sheila posed an immediate danger to herself or others: in other words, was she likely to use the firearms that she clearly had access to. Jeremy explained that Sheila had been treated for depression and was recently diagnosed as a schizophrenic. She had only come out of hospital a few weeks ago.

The officers were puzzled. They wondered why Nevill Bamber had called his son for assistance rather than the police and why Jeremy had tried to contact two local police stations instead of dialling 999 immediately. Bamber dismissed their concerns, claiming that his father didn't like involving outsiders and preferred to keep family matters low key.

Bews spotted a light on downstairs. Glancing up he noticed that two rooms upstairs were also illuminated. The house appeared to be secure with no sign of a break in, but the muffled sound of a distressed dog barking emanated from the house.

Bews enquired whether Sheila could use a gun. Bamber admitted that they had been target-shooting together. He also remembered that he'd left an automatic .22 loaded near the kitchen the previous night. He had been out to shoot rabbits and when he had returned he'd left the gun propped against a wooden settle with a full magazine clip and a box of ammunition lying next to it.

Sergeant Bews had heard enough and instantly called for back up from the Tactical Firearms Unit. The worst case scenario was that there could be four dead bodies and a mentally disturbed female brandishing a gun to deal with. In the meantime he asked that Jeremy draw a plan of the house, illustrating where all the doorways and windows were located.

At 5 am a marksmen squad arrived from Essex Police Tactical Firearms Unit and surrounded the farmhouse. Jeremy was gently guided away by a police officer and taken to a telephone kiosk in the village to call his girl-friend, Julie Mugford, in London. He informed her that a police car would collect her and bring her to Tolleshunt D'Arcy later that morning. He wanted her by his side.

Bamber returned to the scene and sat patiently in a nearby police car with PC Robert Lay, waiting for news of his family. PC Lay noted that Bamber was unusually calm under the circumstances, only occasionally betraying his emotions. Sergeant Adams attempted to make contact with the occupants of White House Farm via a loud hailer from a control point inside the main barn. The disturbing bark of the family dog was the only response he received.

At 6.45 am two police buses arrived carrying additional armed officers and Inspector Ivor Montgomery, the commander of the Tactical Firearms Unit. Montgomery explained to Bamber that his officers would split into two groups. One group would storm the house while the other group would provide cover and containment. At 7.25 am the raid group prepared to storm the property through the kitchen door.

Six marksmen crept towards the house. Acting Sergeant Peter Woodcock swung a sledgehammer several times at the rear door until it burst open in a shower of splinters. Four of the men moved forward while two remained outside to provide cover in the event of an ambush. The first hint of the horror that had gripped White House Farm was Nevill Bamber's bullet-riddled and battered body slumped across an overturned chair in the kitchen, his blood-splattered head slammed face down in the Aga fuel hood.

The officers moved closer to survey the sickening carnage. Nevill's blue pyjama top was saturated with blood and his pyjama bottoms were pulled down around his knees. Dark red pools soaked the floor around him and there was evidence of a violent and frenzied struggle.

Broken crockery, chairs and stools lay scattered across the floor. The large wooden table in the centre of the room had been laid neatly for breakfast but in the struggle a bowl of sugar had been knocked to the floor. The blood stained grains glistened with glass splinters that had fallen from the shattered light fitting above. A trail of blood spots led Woodcock's eye to the telephone receiver resting off the hook on the work surface at the opposite end of the room.

The raid group moved to the foot of the stairs and, using an extended mirror, they could see a hand dangling from a bedroom doorway. They crept slowly up the staircase and found Nevill's wife, June, sprawled on her back with her head propped against the open door. The 61-year-old had sustained multiple shots to her head and the trail of blood leading from a drenched pillow to the door suggested she had tried to drag herself to safety from her bed.

PC Collins was startled by a high-pitched whimper from beneath the mattress. He stooped down and peered underneath the bed frame to find a shih-tzu dog cowering with terror. Behind the animal he could see another annihilated head resting at the foot of the bed.

The corpse was female and she was stretched out on her back. There were two bullet wounds beneath her chin and a .22 rifle lay precariously on top of her with the barrel positioned close to her jaw. He quickly identified the woman as Jeremy's sister, Sheila Caffell. A Bible lay open and face down on the carpet next to her as if it had been deliberately placed there.

PC Collins moved down the landing with two other officers. They flung open the bedroom door and found Sheila's six-year-old twin boys, Nicholas and Daniel, dead in their beds. Both had been shot in the head at point blank range; one of them still had his thumb in his mouth. Ivor Montgomery's radio crackled. He listened intently to the message from the raid group and nodded grimly. The house was clear. Everyone in it had been fatally shot.

Dr Ian Craig, who had worked as the police surgeon for almost 30 years, was summoned to examine the five bodies and to certify their deaths. With him was Chief Superintendent George Harris, head of the Chelmsford division of Essex Police.

Jeremy Bamber stepped out of the car and pleaded with Harris to let him into the house to talk to his father. Harris was forced to break the news that Jeremy's parents were dead. But Bamber continued to plead between sobs as if he hadn't registered the sombre information. Dr Craig fetched a hip flask from his car and offered Jeremy a slug of Scotch to steady his nerves. He suggested they take a walk to help clear his head.

As they walked, Bamber expressed his regret that Sheila had been let out of the psychiatric hospital. He explained that Sheila, who was also adopted, had been staying with their adoptive parents to aid her recovery from a recent mental breakdown. He claimed he had also witnessed a family quarrel the previous evening when June and Nevill had accused Sheila of being an unfit mother and suggested that the twins should be taken into care.

Bamber confessed that he suspected this family disagreement was behind Sheila's outburst with the gun. He said that Sheila had also confided to close family

78

members that she believed her children were evil and that the only way to rid them of such evil was to kill them. As June and Nevill would obviously stand in her way, and had already accused her of being an unfit mother, she would have murdered them too and then turned the gun on herself.

Jeremy thanked Dr Craig for the chat and said he would prefer to continue with the walk alone. As the doctor turned to walk back towards the farmhouse two officers stepped out of an unmarked car. They were Detective Sergeant Stan Jones and his superior, Detective Inspector Bob Miller, from Braintree. Stan Jones glanced beyond Dr Craig and noticed Jeremy Bamber retching in a nearby field. They left him to reflect for a few moments in peace.

The house was swarming with officers. Amidst the mêlée, Stan Jones spotted the head of CID, Supt Taff Jones, who instructed him to take the grieving Jeremy Bamber home.

Bamber refused the offer of a lift and insisted on driving himself home. As he turned the key in the ignition another officer ran towards the Vauxhall Astra and motioned to him to stop. In his arms lay Crispy, the quivering shih-tzu. Stan Jones suggested that he take the dog home with him. But Jeremy's response was to ram the car into gear and release the handbrake. As he accelerated away he told Jones to get rid of the 'fucking thing', saying he's always hated it. Jones was alarmed by Bamber's outburst but put it down to shock rather than intentional malice.

Jones and his colleague, Detective Constable Mick

Clark, followed Jeremy Bamber to his small cottage in Head Street, Goldhanger. On arrival Bamber announced he was hungry and prepared and ate a large fried breakfast under the bewildered gaze of the two officers. He then began his testimony.

In order to piece together the events leading to the massacre Jones and Clark started to unravel the complex Bamber family history. June Bamber was the daughter of wealthy landed farmers, Leslie and Mabel Speakman. June had a sister, Pamela, and both girls had married farmers and continued with the family tradition of farming. June met Nevill, then an agricultural student, at a tennis party. They married in September 1949 and in 1950 they moved into White House Farm, a spectacular Georgian farmhouse decked with ivy and positioned enviably close to the coast. Nevill formed a partnership with his father-in-law and farmed his lands in Goldhanger. After Leslie Speakman's death in 1975 Nevill formed another partnership with his wife, June, in a company called N and J Bamber Ltd.

Leslie Speakman's other business interests were divided up between the Bambers and June's sister Pamela and her husband, Robert Boutflour. These included the Osea Road Caravan Site, which ran from Maldon down to the River Blackwater and was a particularly profitable concern. Nevill and June's other source of income was as a partner in a cooperative of five local farmers known as the North Maldon Growers, a collective that specialised in produce such as peas and corn-on-the-cob.

To the outside world June and Nevill Bamber led an idyllic life, but for them there was something vital missing. They were longing for a child but, despite years of trying, they had had no success. June later discovered that a cyst on one of her ovaries would prevent her from ever conceiving. In 1958 they adopted a seven-month-old baby girl through the Church of England Children's Society. They called her Sheila Jean.

June's fertility problems led to a severe bout of depression and she underwent a course of electroconvulsive therapy at St Andrew's Hospital in Northampton. Following her treatment, June and Nevill adopted a six-month-old boy in July 1961, who they named Jeremy.

Their niece, Ann, remembers fond times with the Bamber children:

'Although me and my brother, David, were a lot older than Sheila and Jeremy, I remember we used to go to tennis parties at their house and we had great fun with them.'

Both Sheila and Jeremy attended Maldon Court, a private preparatory school. At age ten, Sheila was sent away to boarding school in Eastbourne, but she failed to settle and at 13 she moved to another school in Norfolk. David recalls that Sheila developed a wild side as a teenager: 'She loved parties and hankered for London life away from the rural tranquillity of White House Farm.' Through her teenage years Sheila frequently played truant from school and was eventually expelled.

At 16 she moved to London and, after failing at a succession of menial jobs, she enrolled on a modelling course at the Lucie Clayton School. A brief modelling career commenced, with Sheila using the nickname 'Bambi' to fit her new identity. According to Jeremy, Sheila's career was short-lived, since she soon became swept up in an overwhelming tide of drugs and debt.

David remembers that Sheila was an attractive, fun-loving girl:

'She accompanied me to a few young farmers' functions and, in later years, when I married, my wife and I used to visit her in London. She was always thrilled to see us and maintained that link with the country, despite her love of life in the capital and the endless round of parties.'

Possibly one reason for Sheila's lust for life away from White House Farm was her mother's unbending religious propriety. June Bamber became obsessed and preoccupied by pious theological teachings, constantly quoting religious texts and frowning on her teenage daughter's increasing interest in sex. When she stumbled across Sheila indulging in a sexual encounter in the hay she taunted her for her 'sinful behaviour'. During her early adult life Sheila had two abortions and her cousin, David, believed that this affected her mental state in later years. 'She always felt guilty about the abortions and worried that she might not be able to conceive in later years. June Bamber's strict religious attitude coupled with her own fertility problems fuelled her resentment towards her daughter's interest in sex and the ensuing aborted pregnancies.'

By 1977 Sheila was engaged to sculptor Colin Caffell and was expecting his baby. She miscarried but a year later she was pregnant again with the twins and, in June 1979, Nicholas and Daniel were born.

David remembers the arrival of the twins was a turning point for Sheila: 'It was then that it all really started to go wrong for her. She couldn't cope with the twins and relied heavily on June Bamber for practical and financial support.'

Her marriage to Colin failed and Sheila sank into frequent bouts of depression. Gripped by religious fervour, June found her daughter's failed marriage and her previous abortions difficult to come to terms with. Her obsession with Sheila's morality led to a mental breakdown.

Meanwhile, Sheila's own mental health was deteriorating and Dr Hugh Ferguson diagnosed her as suffering from a state of acute psychosis. During her treatment he also discovered that Sheila was displaying symptoms of paranoid schizophrenia and that she felt at times that she was possessed by the Devil.

Dr Ferguson discovered that many of Sheila's delusions about good and evil were linked to her relationship with the overzealous June Bamber. Ferguson continued to treat Sheila for the following two years, but he did not think that Sheila's delusions suggested that she had any propensity towards violence.

In contrast to Sheila, Jeremy was self-assured, ambitious and had a clear sense of direction. Like his sister he hankered after a luxurious lifestyle and preferred to socialise in London. His early years of boarding at Gresham's School on the Norfolk coast provided a mixture of experiences. He was bullied by the other boys for being adopted, but in later life he reflected that his time at Gresham's was a great experience that taught him self-sufficiency.

Nevill Bamber worked hard to groom his adopted son to follow in his own farming footsteps, but Jeremy had other ideas. He was keen to travel and, in 1978, having failed his A Levels, Jeremy spent a year travelling in Australia and New Zealand. In New Zealand he enrolled on a scuba diving course and, when money ran out, he sent a letter home demanding that his parents send him some more cash. There was a second trip to New Zealand, followed by a visit to the Middle East. Once again he ran out of cash but, rather than sending additional funds, Nevill Bamber sent his son a one-way ticket home.

On his return, he was reluctant to settle down to rural life and, much to June's chagrin, he embarked on a relationship with an older, married mother of three. When Suzette Ford's husband learned of the relationship he left her, and Jeremy Bamber moved into her Colchester home at the weekends.

June Bamber admonished Jeremy at every opportunity, moralising that the extra-marital affair and having sex before marriage were mortal sins. In the end it was Suzette who tired of Jeremy and she returned to her husband.

Jeremy reluctantly began to help out on the farm and attend board meetings at the Osea Road Caravan Site, in which he had an eight per cent share. He took an unexpected trip to New Zealand in the middle of the harvest, but on his return he began working full-time at White House Farm.

Nevill rewarded his adopted son's commitment with the rent-free tenancy of a small cottage in Goldhanger, a company car and a salary of £8,750, supplemented by a bonus and a director's fee from the caravan site. Perks of the job also included free bottled gas to heat the cottage, unlimited free use of the telephone, private medical cover and free car fuel and insurance. Despite his father's generosity, Jeremy was never satisfied and hankered after more money to fund a lifestyle that was well beyond his means.

Jeremy also had a new girlfriend, a student teacher called Julie Mugford. Life was becoming more structured and Jeremy appeared to be settling down. He was also given more responsibility at the caravan site and was tasked with collecting the annual site fees. Once collected, the money was normally paid into the bank, but Jeremy suggested that two weeks of the takings were temporarily placed in the office safe.

The office was burgled shortly afterwards and almost one thousand pounds was stolen from the safe. Jeremy's uncle, Robert Boutflour, was suspicious about his adoptive nephew, and later confided in the police that he had, 'Always suspected Jeremy of being responsible for the burglary because of his desire for money.'

Stan Jones and Mick Clark were beginning to build a picture of Jeremy Bamber as an arrogant and reckless young man whose desire for wealth outweighed his social conscience.

His cousin David Boutflour recalled how rude Jeremy was towards his mother, even in front of other people: 'At times he could be absolutely obnoxious to his mother and didn't care who was there to hear it. He was verbally abusive and I think if I had behaved like that towards my mother, then my father would have knocked my head off.'

David's sister, Ann Eaton, remembered Jeremy taunting his mother on several occasions: 'He was always trying to get a reaction out of her and used to bait her about religion. She was very moral and she didn't approve of the way he was living his life, but most of the time she didn't rise to the bait.'

Friends of the family and other employees were also beginning to notice Jeremy's indifference towards the farm and Nevill's increasing irritation with him. Nevill was also becoming aware that his son was becoming more aggressive towards him and he despaired of Jeremy's nonchalant attitude towards the family business. He confided in his secretary Barbara Wilson that Jeremy and Sheila were costing him a lot of money and were full of ingratitude.

Barbara noticed that Nevill was looking increasingly tired. She wondered if he was carrying the burden of a serious illness or was undergoing stress in his personal life which was grinding him down: 'He asked me to promise that I would take care of the farm if anything ever happened to him. I asked him why he was worrying about it but it was some time later before he finally revealed to me what was on his mind. He swore me to secrecy and I didn't utter a word until long after Nevill had died.' Nevill Bamber had been struck by a sense of foreboding and instinct told him that his life would end imminently.

Stan Jones was beginning to feel deeply uneasy. He wondered if Jeremy was responsible for the mass shooting and was simply trying to frame his mentally ill sister. For now, he decided to keep his suspicions to himself and continue to delve into the background to the case.

A member of the family was also beginning to question Jeremy's part in the murder. His cousin, Ann Eaton, who was the daughter of June's sister, Pamela Boutflour, had her own ideas about who was responsible for pulling the trigger: 'After the murders lots of seemingly inconsequential comments suddenly fell into place. Once he told me that in two years' time the caravan park would all be his and that was such a strange thing to say.'

'Another time he announced that he wanted a 12 bore, automatic, five-shot repeater gun. He said he fancied becoming a country squire and doing a bit of shooting. My husband, who knows a bit about shooting, told him it wasn't an appropriate gun for that kind of sport. After the murders it occurred to me that he wanted a five-shot repeater and here we had five people dead. I started to put two and two together.

'My impression was that Jeremy always felt he was hard done by. He complained that he put all the hours in and worked hard, while Sheila managed to get a flat and financial support from June and Nevill without lifting a finger.' June used her director's fee from the caravan site to buy Sheila a flat in London, she paid most of her bills and she bought and delivered her weekly groceries. Jeremy, on the other hand, was expected to start work at 7.30 am and earn every penny of his keep. Ann suspected that the difference in the way they were treated had fuelled his resentment towards his adoptive parents.

On the morning of the tragedy Ann Eaton telephoned Jeremy at the cottage. He was distraught and felt that he had no family left. Ann drove straight over to console him. When Ann arrived she noticed something different about Jeremy's demeanour: 'He looked dark. His pupils were dilated and he had developed a sort of strange cough. I put my arms around him and said, "I'm so sorry Jeremy." He told me that Sheila was responsible for the deaths, but he never seemed to blame himself for leaving the gun out and loaded like other people would have done. There was no remorse. I never saw him shed any tears.'

Shortly after Ann's arrival a police car drew up outside with Julie Mugford. The couple embraced and exchanged a few words. A few hours later Sheila's ex-husband, Colin Caffell, and his girlfriend, Heather Amos, arrived from London. Both were distraught and Colin blamed himself for leaving the twins at White House Farm, but insisted that Sheila would never kill her own children.

Ann Eaton kept the guests supplied with coffee while Jeremy continued giving his statement to detectives. He told them that he had spent the previous day at the farm helping with the harvest. At teatime he had returned to the farmhouse where Nevill and June were telling Sheila that she was an unfit mother and that her children should be taken into care. He recalled that Sheila had sat staring ahead and remained silent throughout.

He explained to the officers that he had spotted some rabbits and decided to load the Anschutz .22 rifle in order to try to shoot the animals. When they escaped he returned with the still-loaded gun and left it on the wooden settle in the kitchen.

Ann Eaton made surreptitious notes of Jeremy's statement and pored over it when she arrived home. It troubled her. Some things just didn't add up. It wasn't protocol to leave a loaded gun lying around and Ann felt sure that Sheila had never fired a gun and would have no idea how to use one.

'Jeremy told the detectives that he enjoyed a good relationship with his father and I knew that this was untrue. There was a great deal of tension between the two men because Jeremy was reluctant to work on the farm and was always trying to persuade his father to fund his extravagant lifestyle.'

Then there was the late night telephone call. Jeremy claimed his father had called him saying that Sheila had gone crazy with a gun, after which the line went dead. Surely either Nevill or Jeremy would have immediately called 999 rather than waste vital time? And why did the police car manage to reach White House Farm before Jeremy, who was only minutes away? He was well known for his fast driving, yet on this occasion he appeared to have crawled at a snail's pace to the farm.

Jeremy told police he had hung back because he feared that Sheila would also attack him with the gun, because they didn't get on. Ann later reflected that, 'If that had been my family at risk, then wild horses wouldn't have stopped me from getting into that house.' To an outsider Jeremy's justifications probably sounded plausible, but

Ann knew that Sheila didn't have much practical experience of firearms and that she would have had great difficulty hitting her targets with every single bullet fired. Yet the killer hadn't missed a single shot and had managed to reload the gun three more times.

Ann's brother David was also having doubts about Jeremy's version of events. He had heard Jeremy explain that he had removed the silencer and telescopic sight from the rifle so that it would fit back into the gun cupboard, but then he had left it on the wooden settle in the kitchen. Boutflour couldn't understand why Bamber had needed to remove the telescopic sight because he knew that the rifle would fit back into the gun cupboard perfectly well with it still fitted. Bamber said that he had left the loaded magazine in the gun but not a loaded bullet in the breech. This struck Boutflour as odd, because if Bamber had fired some shots at rabbits as he claimed to have done then there must have been a bullet in the breech, unless he had removed the magazine and the bullet separately, which would have meant that the magazine was no longer in the gun.

Jeremy was now officially the head of the household and utilised his new authority to order the destruction of the blood-stained carpets and curtains from White House Farm. A new back door was ordered to replace the one destroyed by the forced entry of the police and security alarms were fitted to deter burglars. The farm was home to a number of expensive antiques and once news of the deaths were announced by the media, there was a high risk of potential raids.

At 8.30 pm that day Stan Jones and Mick Clark said their goodbyes. As they left the cottage Jones was troubled by Jeremy's cheerful spirit. As they drove to the debriefing at Witham Police Station Jones kept replaying in his mind Colin Caffell's insistent protestations that Sheila wouldn't have done it. He remembered Jeremy's cruel dismissal of Crispy the dog and the hearty fried breakfast he had enjoyed within hours of hearing his immediate family had been murdered. He was already beginning to suspect that Jeremy was more involved than he cared to admit, but it was still too early for him to voice his suspicions, since they were as yet unsubstantiated.

They arrived at the police station and sat through a half-hour briefing chaired by Detective Chief Inspector Taff Jones. The DCI announced that the cause of the deaths were four murders and a suicide and that they were to gather statements for the coroner as a formality.

Headlines about the model girl, Bambi, who had slain her family, adorned the front pages of the newspapers. But Ann Eaton was surprised by newspaper reports that Sheila was taking drugs. When she questioned Jeremy about this he confirmed that she had been taking hard drugs and added that the police would be able to verify such usage when they 'cut into her fatty tissue.' Ann was taken aback by his remark: 'It just seemed such an awful thing to say about his dead sister. He seemed so nonchalant about her.'

Jeremy appeared to take the media reports and the grisly events of the family massacre in his stride. Apart from one element of the investigation: he refused to formally identify the bodies. But to everyone's surprise, his girlfriend Julie Mugford agreed to perform the task.

Bamber announced that while Julie was identifying the bodies he intended to pay a visit to the family lawyers and accountants to sort out the business and financial affairs and assess the size of his inheritance. Stan Jones was startled that Jeremy was ready to attend to such matters only a day after the shootings.

Jones' suspicions about Jeremy were increasing by the minute, so he decided to further question Julie Mugford about the time when Bamber first called her on the night of the murders. Mugford told him that Jeremy had rung at around 3.30 am, just minutes after calling the police at 3.26 am. Jones wasn't convinced and made a mental note to check the time with Julie's flatmates in London. Itemised telephone bills didn't exist in 1985 and Jones would have to find out by checking with other witnesses who might have been disturbed by the telephone ringing in the flat and had subsequently checked the time. He believed that Bamber may have called Julie before ringing the police and he surmised that this pointed to his guilt. If Bamber was innocent, surely he would have contacted the police without delay ...

Ann offered to go with Jeremy to the solicitors and the accountants but he told her he would rather go alone. So Ann travelled with Julie and waited in the car outside the mortuary for her: 'I didn't want to identify them because I preferred to remember them as they were. All the time Julie was in there I kept wondering if I should have gone in. Eventually Julie came back out and as she climbed in the car she asked if I minded her lighting a cigarette. She said the identification was easier than she thought it would be, that they all looked peaceful, but their heads had been shaved. She told me they were badly bruised and that uncle Nevill looked the worst. I hadn't realised they would have to have their heads shaved and was relieved that I hadn't gone in to see them.'

Stan Jones and Mick Clark attended a briefing called by DCI Taff Jones to discuss the pathologist's report. Dr Vanezis confirmed that all the victims had died from shotgun wounds to the head, which in some cases were fired at point blank range.

He continued, 'Nevill had several gunshot wounds and a number of bruises to his body that all indicated he had put up a fight and struggled quite a bit before death. He had pistol-whipping injuries on his hands, which suggested he was struck by the gun as he tried to defend himself. There was also a curious burn-like injury to his back, which in retrospect indicated that the gun had been pointed into his back at one stage.

'June Bamber also had a number of injuries. The fatal shot was fired while she was on the floor near the door, but her first injuries were inflicted while she was still in bed. June's injuries were not as severe as her husband's but were horrific all the same. The two children had injuries to the head and appeared to have been facing the murderer when they were shot, but they were probably asleep and died instantly.'

'Sheila had two wounds to her neck. One was a contact

wound that penetrated soft tissue, but the second one injured the base of the brain and was fatal. '

Stan Jones listened to the report incredulously. Was it possible that Sheila could have shot herself twice? Dr Vanezis confirmed that the first shot might not have sent Sheila unconscious and that she could have fired a second shot, so suicide could not be ruled out. Stan Jones wondered whether she would have been capable of this when she had already blasted half her jaw away. And if she hadn't fired the second, fatal shot, then that meant that somebody else had.

Dr Vanezis was sickened by the scene: 'I had never seen anything so horrific in terms of such a cold, calculated, callous murder of a family. To think that one person was capable of such a mass killing still sends me cold to this day.'

Stan Jones decided to voice his opinion and told the gathered officers that he believed that Sheila was not responsible for the murders and that the likely culprit was Jeremy Bamber. DCI Taff Jones gritted his teeth, maintaining that all the evidence pointed to it being four murders and a suicide.

Back at Bourntree Cottage in Goldhanger, Jeremy told Ann and his other cousin, Anthony Pargeter, that they were both beneficiaries in his parent's will, to the tune of £1000 and £500. He told them that his parents had far more interests than he had at first thought and quoted what their various properties and assets were worth on the open market.

Ann and Anthony were shocked by the financial and

commercial interests listed in the wills and decided to retire to Ann's home in order to discuss their suspicions in private. Ann's brother, David, joined the discussions and they decided to share their misgivings with the police. The next morning they met with DCI Taff Jones at the Essex police headquarters in Chelmsford. But Taff Jones was in no mood to entertain their suspicions.

Ann says, 'He told us that rounds had been fired and that the rifle was discovered on Sheila's body without its silencer. This meant that the murderer would have had to reload the magazine three times and I pointed out that there was no way that Sheila would have been able to do that. I started to make notes and he suddenly stood up and banged his hands down on the table and snapped, "I don't have to put up with this." We carried on and tried to point out that the gun would have fitted into the gun cupboard with the silencer on so there was no need for Jeremy to remove it the night before like he said he did.'

The family were given short shrift by DCI Taff Jones, and were hastily ushered out by an embarrassed and apologetic Stan Jones. Later that day Taff Jones insisted Stan accompany him on a visit to Bourntree Cottage to see Jeremy Bamber. He was unconvinced by both the family and Stan Jones' suspicions regarding Jeremy Bamber and was set on disproving their theories once and for all.

While they were there, the police informed the family that White House Farm was ready to be reoccupied. Jeremy refused to go back to the house, claiming he could see the faces of his murdered family every time he went near it, so the officers arranged to hand the keys over to Ann Eaton, since she was his closest surviving relative.

Jeremy was already making arrangements to dispose of the family assets in return for cash. He told Ann Eaton that he had arranged for Sotheby's to value the contents, which included numerous antiques.

That evening Ann Eaton and her husband Peter returned to White House Farm for the handover of the keys. Bracing themselves, they stepped inside through the new kitchen door. They had been warned to expect that things would be out of place following the murders and subsequent forensic investigation. In the dining room there were still childish crayon drawings laid out on the table where the twins had left them before going to bed on that fateful night.

Ann was shocked to discover that half the carpet had been removed from June and Nevill's bedroom. The detectives explained that it had been heavily bloodstained from June and Sheila's bodies. Likewise, in the twins' bedroom the blood-splattered mattresses and pillows had been removed and burned. The officers showed the couple how to operate the newly installed burglar alarm and handed over the keys.

The next morning Ann returned alone. It was Saturday and she decided to spend the day cleaning the farm. As she stood at the kitchen sink she noticed some strange smudges on the inside of the window pane. Looking down at the window sill she was sure she could see some blood.

At 11 am her brother David arrived. Ann pointed out

her discoveries and they decided to make their own thorough search of the house in pursuit of clues that may have been overlooked by the police. They were joined by their father Robert Boutfour, who had arranged to meet them at the house for lunch. David made straight for the gun cupboard. He searched methodically through the contents and pulled out a Parker-Hale gun silencer, which was standing on its end in the back left-hand corner.

They took the silencer and several other items from the farm back to Ann's House. Ann's husband, Peter, who was an expert in firearms, looked closely at the silencer; but it was David who noticed that there was something on it. They all moved closer to inspect the silencer. Stuck near the exit hole they could clearly see a blob of coagulated blood. There also appeared to be a minute fleck of paint on the end of the silencer that seemed to match the paintwork around the Aga at White House Farm. It looked like this was the silencer that belonged to the gun used in the murders. But if that was so, why had Sheila removed it before returning upstairs to kill herself in the bedroom. It didn't make sense.

Robert had also made some interesting discoveries during his search of the property that day. He had identified six windows that could have been used by an intruder without showing signs of forced entry. The window bearing the blood smears in the kitchen was among his list of possibilities.

Five days after the killings, Robert and his wife Pamela drove to Maldon Police Station in order to report their suspicions to the duty sergeant. An appointment with

Detective Sergeant Stan Jones was arranged for later that afternoon. They then made their way to White House Farm to meet their daughter, Ann, who was cleaning the house. Shortly after their arrival, Robert and Pamela were surprised to see Jeremy and Julie appear at the door. Ann had invited Jeremy, having realised that he hadn't set foot near the place since the night of the murders.

They all noted that Jeremy was suffering from the shakes and was almost at the point of collapse. Ann later commented that, 'Although he seemed unwell it still riled me that he went straight over to his father's chair and sat in it. It was like a lack of respect for Uncle Nevill, because nobody but him ever sat in that seat.'

Ann offered to take Jeremy on a tour of the house, which Jeremy insisted Julie accompany him on. Julie was reluctant and tearful but, without saying a word, he clasped her hand and she rose to follow him. He looked drawn and pale and was unsteady on his feet. Jeremy noted that items were missing from the rooms, so Ann explained that she had stored the valuables in chests and that they were safe. As they moved upstairs, Ann felt Jeremy physically resist, holding back as if nervous of entering the upstairs bedrooms. He stood in the doorway of his parents' bedroom speechless and staring.

'Then,' Ann described, 'I brought him to Sheila's room and he stood away from the door and he wouldn't go in. He stood bolt upright and sort of zombified. And I saw this look in his eyes, really dark. I got hold of his arm and I said, "Come on, Jeremy, nothing happened in here," and I pulled him in. After that we were going to the twins room and he did something extraordinary. He seemed to hunch over and start tiptoeing. I said, "I've changed things around in this room, Jeremy," and then he quite easily came in.'

Jeremy seemed to regain his composure quickly and started to take stock of what was missing from the property. He telephoned the police to report that his father's wallet, containing cash and credit cards, was missing. Then he unplugged the video-recorder in the sitting room and carried it to his car, claiming that it belonged to him. The family looked on astounded.

That evening Detective Sergeant Stan Jones arrived at the Eatons' home to collect the silencer that Robert and Pamela Boutflour had told him about. He took a closer look and could clearly see something resembling congealed blood at the knurled end. There was also a reddish-brown paint mark ingrained in the knurl and a small grey hair attached to a scratch in the metal. Jones was ill-prepared for the task but, realising that the evidence needed some protection, he asked Peter Eaton for the cardboard tube from the centre of some kitchen towel roll and slid the silencer inside it. He bent over the ends to secure it into position and took it back to CID.

Jones placed the new evidence in front of the scene of crime officer, Inspector Ron Cook, and pointed out the hair, the paint, the scratch and the blood. Cook looked unconvinced. He deduced that the blood could have come from a farm animal and that the hair and the paint could have easily lodged onto the silencer at any time. He was sceptical and probably unwilling to depart from DCI Taff Jones' official line that Sheila was responsible for the four murders and a suicide. Jones hadn't given up yet, though. He would keep pressing gently until someone agreed to submit the silencer for forensic examination.

Ann Eaton busied herself in the days following the murders by trying to look after everyone else and to take care of the farmhouse. But an emotional telephone call to a relative to discuss the funeral arrangements reduced her to tears. In a moment of vulnerability she called Jeremy at the cottage. He drove over to her home in Little Totham immediately and in an uncharacteristic display of emotion he wrapped his arms around her and comforted her.

Ann later regretted her moment of weakness in front of Jeremy: 'I've vexed myself many a time for allowing myself to show my vulnerable side to Jeremy. It was the only time that I succumbed to his manipulative charm.'

She reflected on Jeremy's sudden warmth towards her. Days after the murder he had sent her a bouquet of flowers with a card bearing the message: 'Thank you for all your loving – Jeremy.'

Until a year before the killings Jeremy had always behaved coolly towards his cousin, resenting her involvement in the caravan site and pouring cold water on her business propositions. Without warning, his attitude changed and he began complimenting her input and, for the first time ever, he sent her a birthday card.

'When I rang to thank him for the card he laughed and replied: "Well, I am your favourite cousin, aren't I?" and I was really taken aback.' He even began inviting me over to the cottage to use his sunbed. Jeremy adored his sunbed and often joked to people that he had been abroad when in fact his tan was acquired in the spare bedroom. I was never sure why he kept offering me the use of his sunbed, but he always used to joke that there was no lock on the door. It was all quite strange.'

A week after the murders Stan Jones was idly flicking through the photographs taken at the scene of the crime. Suddenly, something caught his eye in the picture in front of him. The paint on the silencer seemed to be a perfect match to the reddish brown surrounding the Aga.

Jones wasted no time and contacted Jeremy to ask permission to go back into White House Farm. He said that they needed some room measurements for the inquest. Accompanied by Bob Miller and Ron Cook he returned to the farm. Cook carefully scraped a sample of the red paint from the mantelpiece above the Aga. Jones noticed two gouge marks in the paintwork on the underside of the mantelpiece and felt his heart beat faster. They looked like they had occurred recently and were the result of two heavy blows.

The funerals took place just over a week after the deaths. Hundreds of mourning villagers attempted to cram into the church of St Nicholas in Tolleshunt D'Arcy to pay their respects to the family. The press hovered on the road, waiting to catch on camera the chief mourners. Jeremy Bamber obligingly walked slowly behind the coffins, leaning heavily on Julie. They were followed by Colin Caffell, the Eatons and the Boutflours. The Reverend Bernard Robson spoke of the sense of loss and shock that had swept over the community and reminded them of the family's commitment to religion.

The service was followed by a cremation, which Jeremy had insisted upon. The rest of the family were reluctant to cremate the five and Ann was confused by Jeremy's insistence.

She says, 'We knew that Auntie June and Uncle Nevill wanted to be buried, but Jeremy said he wanted them cremated because their bodies weren't whole. Colin stepped in and insisted that the twins would be buried at a separate ceremony at Highgate Cemetery in north London, but the rest were cremated.

'We first learned that Jeremy wanted the bodies to be cremated when a relative asked if she could have Auntie June's engagement ring and Jeremy refused, saying he wanted it cremated with her. The rest of the family weren't happy about it but Jeremy had the final word.'

David Boutflour was troubled by Jeremy's demeanour on the day of the funerals. 'When the hearse left, Jeremy turned around in the funeral car and gave everyone in the car behind a huge grin. For the cameras he appeared to be upset and wavering on his feet but in private he was smiling and showed no sadness.'

To the viewing public Jeremy Bamber looked like a man reaching the end of his tether. He stumbled as he walked, leaning on Julie for support, but once he was back in the private confines of the car he turned to Julie and said: 'Aren't I a good actor?'

Jeremy seemed to recover very quickly from the massacre at White House Farm. Even before the funerals, he and Julie had two guests staying with them, Julie's friend, Liz Rimmington, and a gay associate of Jeremy's called Brett Collins, who he had met in New Zealand. After the cremation and the wake at Goldhanger, Jeremy suggested that he take Julie, Liz, Brett and two friends, Andy and Karen Bishop, who were visiting from London, for a meal.

Julie said she wasn't in the mood but Jeremy persuaded her to join the party. They spent the evening in high spirits drinking cocktails, wine and champagne with their meal at a small restaurant in Burnham-on-Couch. When he arrived home Jeremy rewound the video to watch the news bulletins of the funerals. He was annoyed to discover that the machine had failed to record the news and ventured out early the following morning to buy a full set of newspapers to keep up to date with the coverage.

The week after the funerals Jeremy offered to take Brett and Julie to Amsterdam for a couple of days. He was enjoying the attention he was receiving from them both and had joked to his friend, Andy Bishop, that he was secretly pleased that he was at the centre of a tug-of-love triangle between Brett and Julie.

With Jeremy safely out of the way in Holland, Ann decided to employ her own detective skills and search Jeremy's cottage for clues that indicated his hand in the killings at White House Farm. It didn't take her long to stumble across something suspicious. Leaning against the fence by the back door was June Bamber's red bicycle. The bike had been reported missing from the farm following the killings. The wheels were coated with a yellowish mud and Ann realised that this could have been Jeremy's getaway vehicle on the night of the murders. By escaping across the fields, he would have prevented anyone from spotting him and blowing his alibi.

Ann immediately contacted the police to report her discovery. A couple of days later she returned to White House Farm with her father to re-examine the kitchen fanlight window. There were still some watery blood-like marks on the glass and the sill.

They decided to try an experiment to see if someone could slither through the window and then close it without detection. They discovered that you could set the catch from the outside and by pushing the window the catch would fall into the locked position, securing it firmly. Again, Ann contacted Witham police to inform them that it was possible for someone to leave the premises and make it appear as if there was no sign of entry or exit. Ann and her father suspected that Jeremy had slaughtered his family and then left by the window in order to make it look like the murders had been committed from within.

Three weeks after the death of his parents Jeremy was making arrangements to sell their valuables. He loaded his car with their treasured paintings, ornaments and collectables in order to take them to Sotheby's to be valued and catalogued. Robert Boutflour added it to his list of misdemeanours to mention to the police.

Julie Mugford was celebrating her 21st birthday in style. Jeremy and Brett joined her for a family dinner party at a restaurant near Colchester. Throughout the evening Julie noticed the easy familiarity and intimacy between her lover and his friend. Sometimes she wondered if Jeremy acted affectionately towards Brett for effect. People in the village gossiped that Jeremy was bisexual but she had never believed it. However, she was beginning to feel uncomfortable and at times excluded by the tactile bond evident between the two men. Brett stood up to raise a toast to Julie's coming of age and to wish a happy future 'for the engaged couple'. At the mention of engagement Jeremy exploded, emphasising clearly that they had no plans to marry. Julie was embarrassed by his reaction and the next morning returned to London in tears.

Feeling alienated and distraught, Julie confided in her friend Susan Battersby the following evening. She had kept Jeremy's evil secret for long enough and told Susan that, while Jeremy had not committed the murders himself, he had paid someone else to do it.

Susan was stunned by the news. She had never liked Jeremy and had always felt there was something shifty about him. But surely he wasn't so callous that he could wipe out his entire family?

Julie swore her friend to secrecy and revealed how Jeremy had confided in her that he was going to hire a hit man to do the job for him. Julie knew she should tell the police, but confessed to her friend that she still loved Bamber and couldn't bear the thought of him going to prison.

Susan was torn between loyalty to her friend and her nagging conscience. She had promised Julie that she wouldn't utter a word to betray her confidence, but the revelations weighed heavily on her mind. Susan was also aware that Jeremy had rekindled a passionate love affair with his former girlfriend, Virginia Greaves. The affair was the final straw for Julie who had stood by Jeremy and supported him through the dark days following the murders. The confidences which were expected to be maintained by both Julie and her friend Susan would have been too much of a burden for anyone to carry: Julie was beginning to crack.

In the end, it was Jeremy's arrogance and philandering with another woman that prompted Julie to tell another close friend, Liz Rimmington, that Jeremy had murdered his family.

Julie told Liz that Jeremy had been plotting to kill his family for eight months. On learning this, Liz told Julie that she should to go straight to the police for her own safety. But Julie was still torn, and refused to betray Bamber to the police.

Although Julie felt unable to tell the police, she could no longer keep the terrible burden of Jeremy's secret to herself. Soon after confiding in Liz, Julie told her friends Karen and Andy Bishop that Jeremy felt no sorrow over the deaths of his family and, when he discovered a letter from June apologising for the way she had sometimes treated him, he laughed and said he was glad she was dead. Julie feared that Jeremy was a psychopath whose driving force through life was his obsession with money.

Several weeks had passed since the family had handed over the silencer to the police for forensic examination. Robert Boutflour was growing tired and frustrated with the police's apathetic response to the mounting evidence against Jeremy Bamber. He felt it was time to take his concerns to the top.

Boutflour contacted Essex's Assistant Chief Constable (Crime), Peter Simpson, and explained why Sheila could not have been responsible for the murders and her apparent suicide and that Jeremy was the likely culprit. Simpson promised Robert Boutflour that Detective Superintendent Jim Kineally, from Chelmsford headquarters, would reinvestigate the case with immediate effect.

Stan Jones was preparing for a night out with his wife when the telephone rang. He was urgently required to call Liz Rimmington. Instinctively, Jones sensed that any information Rimmington might have was related to Julie Mugford coming forward.

Still wearing his casual clothes, Jones jumped into his car and drove up the A12 to Colchester, where Julie was staying with Liz. There was no time for pleasantries and Stan Jones got straight to the point when he arrived, asking if Jeremy had committed the crimes. The answer was consistent with his longstanding suspicions.

During the journey to the police station, Julie confessed that she couldn't live with the burden of Jeremy's secret any longer. She was ready to make a statement.

At 7 am on Sunday, September 8, the doorbell rang at Sheila's flat in Maida Vale. Jeremy answered the door. Behind him Brett Collins lay naked in one of the beds. A group of detectives were gathered outside. Detective Chief Inspector Taff Jones stepped forward and told him he was being arrested on suspicion of murdering his family.

Two hours later Jeremy was at Chelmsford Police Station turning out his belongings onto the desk. After breakfast and a cup of tea, at 11 am Jeremy was led to the interview room.

Jeremy was questioned about his relationship with his mother and about whether he had baited her regarding her religion. He told the interviewing officer that he had a mixed relationship with his mother that had become more amicable during the six months prior to her death. Then the interview moved to the events of that night and the gun. DCI Jones asked Jeremy about his conversation with Julie earlier in the evening. Had he said words to the effect of, 'Tonight's the night'? Jeremy denied that he had. Had he planned over several months to get rid of his parents, Sheila and the twins? Jeremy denied this too. Had he killed all five members of his family? Jeremy vehemently denied doing so.

During her statement, Julie Mugford confessed to her part in a burglary at the Osea Road Caravan Site earlier that year. She told Detective Stan Jones that Jeremy had burgled the office and stolen £980 from the safe. Her role was to act as lookout. When Jeremy was later questioned about the burglary he admitted it and said that he had done it to prove a point to the other directors and staff that security was too lax.

During his interview Bamber also admitted to selling marijuana to a hitchhiker. But when questioned about the death of his family and any motives he might have had for killing them, Bamber was steadfast. He categorically denied any involvement.

Meanwhile, officers were dispatched to search Jeremy Bamber's cottage, where they seized equipment for growing marijuana. They also returned with June Bamber's red bicycle.

At a case conference the following morning Stan Jones itemised the reasons why he believed that Jeremy Bamber was responsible for the White House Farm killings. He noted that from the outset Jeremy was indifferent to the deaths of his family and any emotion he had shown seemed insincere.

Julie Mugford claimed that Bamber had told her he managed to make himself sick on the day of the murders by thinking of the death of his favourite pet dog. He believed that by vomiting he would convince onlookers that he was distressed and suffering from shock. Julie had also alleged that Bamber had been plotting the murders for eight months. Then there was the factual evidence that Sheila was a frail woman whom the family claimed had no knowledge of guns. Was it really possible that she had overpowered Nevill Bamber, loaded a gun and shot four people before turning the gun on herself? The house was a bloodbath and yet Sheila's feet and legs were remarkably clean when her body was discovered. Surely she would have been covered in blood if she was the murderer?

Finally the day Stan Jones had been waiting for arrived. It was his turn to interview Bamber. Detective Constable Mick Clark and Bamber's lawyer, Bruce Bowler, sat in.

The first session lasted three days and concentrated

largely on Bamber's relationship with Julie Mugford and his adoptive parents. Bamber continued to deny that he felt ill-treated by his parents and wanted to kill them to acquire their money. When Jones asked why Julie Mugford would make all this up, Bamber, claimed that she had a motive for doing so, namely jealousy. He claimed that because he had jilted her, she didn't want anyone else to have him and so wanted him to be put behind bars.

But Stan Jones persisted, stating that Jeremy had told Julie that he would go to White House Farm for supper, when they were all there, and put something in their drinks to make them sleep well. He claimed he would use gin and vodka on the floor, set fire to the house, and the police would believe that his father had accidentally set the house on fire with a cigarette end when he'd fallen asleep in his chair. The fire would destroy all the evidence. Jeremy denied that he had said any such thing.

The police also questioned Jeremy's close friend, Brett Collins. He told them that he had met Bamber in Auckland in 1981 and that they had formed a close friendship. He revealed that, unbeknown to Julie, Jeremy had been two-timing her with other women and, although he was close to Julie, he had no intention of marrying her. Brett described Bamber as vacant, very upset and shocked in the first few weeks after the murders.

Another pawn in the White House Farm massacre was self-employed plumber and central heating engineer, Matthew MacDonald. He was arrested by two armed officers, after Julie Mugford named him as the hit man Jeremy had hired to shoot his family. MacDonald was an associate of Bamber's. They had first met in the Frog and Beans pub in Colchester in 1981. Their dealings with each other were mainly drug-related as the two men often smoked grass together. MacDonald told the police that he hadn't seen or spoken to Jeremy Bamber since December 1984 and he had a cast iron alibi for the night of the murders. After further police checks, MacDonald was free to go.

Another of Bamber's associates at the Frog and Beans, Charles Marsden, told detectives that Jeremy was flash with his money, particularly around women. He also related a conversation he had had with Bamber in December 1984. Jeremy had told him that his family were getting together for Christmas drinks, which Marsden knew was unusual for them. Bamber later confided that if the house burned down over Christmas, then everything would be his. 'I thought it was a strange thing to say, but at the time I didn't pay much attention to it,' said Marsden.

Charles Marsden was also able to throw some light on Bamber's ambiguous sexuality. He recalled that Bamber had numerous one-night stands and revelled in trawling London night clubs, such as Stringfellows, to seduce women. Bamber enjoyed several brief sexual encounters with strangers.

Stan Jones was becoming increasingly frustrated. He was sure Bamber was merely playing a mental game of cat and mouse and that somewhere there was evidence that would nail him. Interviewing was a laborious process in 1985. The police had to write down all the questions and answers when interviewing a suspect and, as Jones recalled, 'He had time to think while we were writing the questions and answers down. He would answer one question and then have time to anticipate the next one before you had finished writing down his answer. He was always ahead of us.'

One area where Stan Jones was able to catch Jeremy Bamber out was on the order of his phone calls on the night of the murders. He initially told the police that he had telephoned them first and then Julie Mugford. When interviewed a week earlier by DCI Taff Jones he made a statement that he telephoned Julie first and then the police, and when questioned again by Stan Jones he reverted to his original statement.

Jones believed that his confusion over the sequence of events and the times indicated that he was being dishonest and that if he was innocent he would probably have contacted the police for help before telephoning Julie. Julie's flatmate, Susan Battersby, told police that she was woken by the telephone ringing and when she checked the clock it was 3.15 am. The police had logged Jeremy's call to Chelmsford station at 3.26 am. If Susan's evidence was accurate, it proved that Jeremy had called Julie before contacting the police.

Something else was troubling Stan Jones. Bamber had claimed that his father had made a desperate call to him pleading for help. When the police stormed the farmhouse they found the telephone off the hook in the kitchen. Forensics showed that Nevill Bamber had first been injured upstairs and then, after a violent struggle, he was killed downstairs. If Jeremy's claim of his father's phone call was true, why was the telephone clean? There wasn't a drop of blood on it, yet Nevill Bamber had already been injured upstairs and would have been bleeding when he made the call.

When questioned about June Bamber's red bicycle, which had been found at his cottage in Goldhanger, Jeremy said he had borrowed it a few days before the murders but did not elaborate as to why. Stan Jones decided to question him about Robert Boutflour's window theory, an allegation that was supported by Julie Mugford, who claimed that Bamber had told her he had identified windows which provided access without detection.

Bamber admitted that on occasion he had used a knife to open the downstairs bathroom window to enter the house. Jones suggested that he had done this on the night of the murders and that after the shootings he had escaped via the kitchen fanlight window and then released the catch to close it securely. Bamber was still adamant that he wasn't involved in any way in the murders.

On Friday, September 13, Jeremy Bamber appeared before the Magistrates' Court in Chelmsford charged with the theft of money from the Osea Road Caravan Site. He was bailed by the court and left without answering any of the questions fired at him by waiting reporters. For now Jeremy Bamber was a free man. Julie Mugford, on the other hand, was in protective police custody.

At the end of December Detective Sergeant Stan Jones, DCI Taff Jones and Assistant Chief Constable Peter Simpson drove to London, where they presented the Deputy Director of Public Prosecutions with their case against Jeremy Bamber. The department was satisfied that a prima facie case existed and that there was sufficient evidence for Bamber to be charged with murder. The only problem was that Bamber had left the country to holiday in St Tropez with Brett Collins. Stan Jones rang several travel agents and discovered that they had purchased open-ended ferry tickets, so there was no way of knowing when they would return. Special Branch at Dover were alerted to watch out for them and to contact Essex Police without delay if they were found. The call came a week later. Jeremy and Brett were detained at Dover on their return from France.

While Jeremy and Brett sat in the interview room believing they were waiting to be questioned about their duty free allowances, a detective sergeant and a detective constable dashed over from Kent Police. They informed Bamber that he was being detained on suspicion of murder and cautioned him.

Detective Sergeant Stan Jones, Detective Inspector Bob Miller and Detective Constable Mick Clark were on the M20 hurrying as fast as they could to reach Dover. They arrived at the docks at 5.45 pm. This was the moment Stan Jones had been waiting for. He marched up to Jeremy Bamber, placed his hand on his shoulder and told him he was being arrested for the five murders of his family and would be taken to Essex to be formally charged.

Bamber was cautioned but barely responded. They arrived back at Essex Police headquarters in Chelmsford at around 10.15 pm. Jeremy was formally charged on five counts of murder. It was almost two months since the massacre at White House Farm.

Jeremy Bamber appeared before magistrates at Maldon the next day and was remanded in custody at Norwich jail for nine days. Although no application for bail was made, his solicitor told the bench that his client had consistently and vehemently denied any involvement in the killings.

News of Bamber's court appearance was splashed across the front pages of the papers. Bamber knew that he would need a specialised and high-profile criminal lawyer to guide him through the tangled and highly publicised court proceedings. His first choice, Sir David Napley, who had a reputation for successfully defending challenging cases, was unable to take Bamber's case on a legal aid basis. Instead he recommended that one of his partners, a tenacious young lawyer called Paul Terzeon, take on the case.

Terzeon visited Bamber at Norwich prison and found him to be an affable, intelligent young man. Bamber continued to protest his innocence and wanted Terzeon to declare in court that the police didn't have a reliable case against him.

Terzeon pored over the prosecution papers and was concerned by the strength of Julie Mugford's witness statements. Trying to argue to magistrates that the police didn't have a case was highly unlikely to persuade them and could land Bamber in even more hot water.

He discussed the case at length with Napley and the two decided that the best option was to go for a paper committal to trial. This would prevent any of the evidence being revealed and tested in front of the magistrates and would give the prosecution less of a chance to identify and rectify any holes in their case.

In the meantime, Terzeon engaged the services of forensic pathologist Professor Bernard Knight, of the University of Wales, to ascertain whether Sheila was responsible for the killings. Another forensic expert, Dr Patrick J Lincoln, was also working on the case, tasked with identifying the blood in the gun silencer. DNA tests were not available in 1985, so the closest evidence scientists could offer was a blood type. Lincoln had disappointing news for Bamber's defence team. The results of the tests he had conducted confirmed that the blood that had blown back into the silencer matched Sheila Caffell's blood type.

This evidence strongly suggested that Sheila had been shot while the silencer was still attached to the rifle. As the weapon had been discovered without the silencer attached, it was unlikely that she had shot herself once with it on, removed it, placed it in the cupboard and returned upstairs to shoot herself a second time. Dr Lincoln's evidence indicated that Sheila had been murdered along with the rest of her family.

The date for the trial was set and Geoffrey Rivlin QC was instructed by Napley's firm to act for Jeremy Bamber at the trial. The junior barrister working on the case was Edmund Lawson, who had a well-earned reputation as a workaholic who thrived when he was pushed to the limits. Bamber's impressive legal team would need every ounce of tenacity and legal argument to pull apart the prosecution case.

Their most pressing concern was to deal with the blood evidence on the silencer. They asked every surviving member of the Bamber family to submit to a blood test. The result was that the blood of Jeremy's uncle, Robert Boutflour, matched the blood group found on the silencer. This gave the defence the possibility of casting doubt on the blood evidence.

Sheila would also have had to remove the silencer to kill herself, because her arms weren't long enough to reach the trigger once the rifle was positioned under her chin. The defence expert, Professor Bernard Knight, emphasised that it would be extremely difficult for a crazed assailant to set up a scene that looked like Sheila's suicide. Many of Sheila's friends were aware of her deep underlying unhappiness and the defence team felt there was a strong possibility that she may have contemplated suicide.

Sheila often told friends that she enjoyed a steady, solid relationship with her adoptive father, but suffered a strained relationship with her devoutly religious adoptive mother. She said June Bamber admonished her for sleeping with men and had told her that she had lost her soul. Sheila rarely mentioned Jeremy other than to say that they had little in common.

She confided to friends that her troubled relationship with June had spurred her to trace her natural mother. In the autumn of 1981 she contacted the Church of England Children's Society, which had placed her with the Bamber family when she was a baby in 1958. A year later she traced and met her natural mother, who travelled from Canada to visit her. The reunion brought Sheila immense joy and helped her to temporarily distance herself from June Bamber's religious fervour.

The defence team decided to pay close attention to the medical evidence of the mental instability that Sheila had gradually developed over a period of years. Her friends described her as an insecure and lonely woman, following her divorce from Colin Caffell. She doted on her children but found the responsibilities of motherhood daunting and was grateful to her ex-husband for sharing the burden. She also sought the help of social services and admitted to suffering from periodic temper tantrums and episodes of self-harm.

There was testimony that Sheila had displayed other violent outbursts in the past. Her Iranian boyfriend, Freddie Emami, once saw her become hysterical during a telephone conversation with a friend. He told the police that Sheila believed that the phone was bugged by the CIA: 'She became like someone possessed, ranting and raving. She was striking herself and beating the wall with her fists. I tried to calm her but she didn't seem to hear me. I became extremely frightened, not only for her but for myself.'

Sheila also told people that she was hearing voices and that God was instructing her to put the world to rights.

'She was behaving like a person possessed, rambling about the Devil and God,' Emami told detectives the day after the murders.

This frenzied outburst, just five months before she died, provided Bamber's defence team with substantial evidence that Sheila was capable of erratic and irrational behaviour. However, several psychiatrists stated clearly that the clinical diagnosis on Sheila's files did not support any theory that she could erupt into mindless and murderous violence that would cause her to annihilate her family.

The other problems Bamber's defence team would face in court were based on circumstantial evidence. There were minimal signs of gun residue on Sheila's hands, yet she would have had to load the gun three times during the massacre. This would have left much larger traces of lead on her hands and it was likely that the small amount she did have had settled on her from the atmosphere.

Her surviving family claimed that she was unfamiliar with firearms, yet every one of the 25 bullets fired, bar one, hit their target. Was it really possible that someone so unaccomplished with guns could achieve such a remarkable result?

Forensic evidence proved that Nevill Bamber had put up a strenuous fight, but Sheila was a slight and fragile woman whose co-ordination and responses were affected by her heavy medication. Therefore, it was improbable that she would have been able to physically overpower him.

During the struggle in the kitchen, light fittings and crockery had been smashed to the floor leaving a thick trail of sharp fragments and sticky blood. Yet when Sheila was found upstairs her feet, legs and hands were relatively clean and her manicured fingernails were in perfect condition. Her body also looked as though it had been carefully arranged with an open Bible placed strategically on the floor next to her.

A week before the trial a highly-regarded psychiatrist expressed his own doubts about Jeremy Bamber's mental stability. He told the defence lawyers that in his opinion Bamber displayed several symptoms of a classic psychopath. He was concerned by Bamber's resolute belief that he was wholly innocent. The psychiatrist explained that in a psychopath's mind the memory of the crime is often forgotten. He believed that Jeremy Bamber had murdered his family and pushed the heinous memory of it to the back of his mind, convincing himself that he was innocent. The news was a blow for Bamber's barrister, Geoffrey Rivlin QC.

On Thursday, October 2 1986, Anthony Arlidge QC opened the case for the prosecution at Chelmsford Crown Court. He outlined how Bamber was due to inherit a sizeable fortune in the event of his parents' and sister's deaths. Arlidge relayed Bamber's version of events that night and revealed how police responding to the incident had overtaken him on the way and noted that he was driving slowly to the scene. They commented amongst themselves on his lack of urgency, despite the severity of the situation.

The prosecution also had evidence that he had telephoned his girlfriend, Julie Mugford, approximately 25 minutes before calling the police to report the incident. Julie had also told police that he had been plotting to kill his family for several months and that he had called her earlier that evening to say, 'Tonight's the night.'

Anthony Arlidge also drew the jury's attention to how Bamber had entered and later left the farmhouse, while managing to ensure it appeared locked and secure. The prosecution claimed he had used the ground floor bathroom window to enter the property. When a forensic expert examined the catch, he found scratch marks in the paintwork. The catch had been painted earlier in the summer so the marks were recent. Two months after the murders a hacksaw blade was found outside, near the window. The scratches on the window catch matched the spacing of the teeth on the hacksaw blade. The Prosecution believed that Bamber had used the blade to force the catch open to gain entry to the house.

Arlidge described to the court how Bamber had taken the gun and shot the two little boys in their bedroom. He then shot his mother, June Bamber. Nevill Bamber had been shot several times and had obviously put up a tremendous struggle taking him from the bedroom to the kitchen below. Arlidge asserted that it had to have been a man who had been fighting with him, probably a young man. Which is why, Arlidge said, Sheila could not have committed the murders and it had to have been Jeremy.

The Prosecution was sure that he had exited the property via a fanlight window in the kitchen. The window had smudges of blood on it and the family housekeeper, Jean Bouttell, had also noted that several items around the sink had been moved from their usual position. Julie Mugford later told the police that Bamber had confided in her that he had discovered a way of getting in and out of the house without detection.

Julie's mother, Mary, recalled that Bamber had told her during Easter in 1985 that he had heard that his mother was thinking of changing the will in favour of the twins. Bamber had, according to Julie, often joked about committing the perfect murder after he heard this.

Then there was the silencer that had been found by David Boutflour in the gun cupboard under the stairs. A blob of congealed blood on the end of the silencer had been tested forensically and matched Sheila Caffell's blood group. Traces of red paint on the silencer were also matched to paintwork on the underside of the mantelpiece above the Aga.

The jury of seven men and five women were shown photo albums crammed with evidential pictures of the horrific scene at White House Farm. They were also shown the murder weapon and told that, according to Sheila's family, she had little knowledge of guns.

Arlidge gave the jury an impression of Bamber's character and attitude towards the death of his family. He told of Julie's claim that, only hours after the murders, when she arrived to be at Jeremy's side, he chuckled and said, 'I should have been an actor.' PC Stephen Myall recalled that Bamber had 'seemed remarkably calm' as they waited for armed back up to arrive and had no sense of wanting to hurry things along. After the murders, Bamber splashed out on expensive holidays and restaurants and sought legal advice to quickly ascertain the size of his inheritance. Police and members of the family noted that his behaviour was uncharacteristic of someone who was supposedly mourning the tragic loss of their family in gruesome circumstances.

The prosecution appeared to have a cast iron case, but there were flaws in their evidence gathering. Crucial exhibits had been mishandled and the scene of crime officer, Detective Inspector Ronald Cook, had to explain to the court how a grey hair attached to the silencer had gone missing in transit to the laboratory. Another key error made by the police was that the murder weapon had been handled by officers who were not wearing protective gloves. Sheila's hand had also been moved before the police photographer arrived and the Bible lying next to Sheila was never tested for fingerprints. The police had failed to take swabs from her hands and feet and the plastic bags encasing them had never been forensically tested.

Barbara Wilson, Nevill Bamber's secretary at the farm, was called to give her evidence. She described how Jeremy had asked her to increase the insurance cover on several of the farmhouse contents because they were underinsured. In the weeks following the killings she recalled how Bamber had instructed her to clear the office of any reminders of his father. She described his manner as 'a bit arrogant and a bit nasty'.

When cross-examined by Rivlin, Barbara Wilson explained that she was in no doubt as to Jeremy's demeanour: 'When someone comes upstairs, sits in a chair with his feet on the desk and swivels round and tells me in the manner that he told me to clear things out, I am not mistaken.'

Prior to the trial Barbara Wilson had been weighed down by guilt. She had promised Nevill Bamber that she wouldn't tell a soul when he confided in her that he had a strong feeling that his days were numbered.

'I'd noticed that Mr Bamber had started to look ill and I gently questioned him about what was worrying him. He told me he had to get his affairs in order, that he had great worries and that he didn't think that he would be here for very long. I asked him if he meant that he was going to die through illness and he said, no, there were other ways and means and that he would probably have some sort of a shooting accident.

'I put two and two together and told him to go to the police and he said that he would get all his affairs in order and then sort it out. In the meantime he made me promise that I wouldn't repeat anything he had told me to anyone.'

Now she felt certain that if she had acted on Nevill's secret revelations, the family might still be alive. The police tried to present Barbara Wilson's information as further proof that Jeremy had pre-planned the murders, but Bamber's defence lawyers dismissed it as inadmissible hearsay evidence.

Five days into the trial the prosecution presented their star witness, Julie Mugford. She was 22 years old and had been separated from Bamber for just over 12 months. Julie told the jury how she and Bamber had first met when she was working as a waitress at a pizza restaurant in Colchester. It was a holiday job to pay her way through Goldsmiths' College in London where she was studying to be a teacher. Bamber was working in the restaurant as a cocktail barman and invited her to accompany him to a party being hosted by the restaurant owners.

The relationship flourished and Bamber took Julie to White House Farm to meet his parents. But June disapproved of Julie spending weekends with Jeremy at his cottage in Goldhanger and confronted her about their sexual relationship. Julie ignored June's cruel jibes about her loose morals and a few months later she moved into the cottage with Jeremy. She spent the college term living with flatmates in London but the rest of the time she spent with Jeremy in Goldhanger.

Julie told the court how Jeremy's bitterness towards his family festered until he finally killed them. She described how Jeremy resented the way his parents tried to run his life and told him who he could and couldn't see. She said he was jealous that Sheila had been given a luxurious flat in Maida Vale and that her lifestyle was funded by Nevill and June, while he had to slave on the family farm for every penny. When she asked him why he didn't just get out and walk away from it all he replied that he had 'too much to lose'.

The jury listened as Julie relayed how Jeremy had repeatedly justified killing his parents. She said he felt his father was getting on and losing his touch, that his mother was mad and that he would be putting her out of her misery. He also said that Sheila was mad and had nothing to live for and that the twins were emotionally disturbed and unbalanced by their upbringing. Julie didn't believe he was serious until he began plotting ways to kill them.

Julie alleged that his suggested methods included drugging the family with tranquillisers and setting fire to the farm. He abandoned the second idea when he discovered that the insurance payout would be minimal.

His other idea was to shoot the family and use Sheila as the scapegoat. She claimed that he had told her he had killed some rats on the farm with his bare hands to test his courage and ability to kill in cold blood.

Julie described the events leading up to the murders. She explained how she had spent the weekend prior to the killings with Jeremy at the cottage. She noticed June Bamber's red bicycle outside the back door, but despite his claims that he had borrowed it for Julie's use, she later recalled that he had once mentioned the bike as a potential mode of transport in his murder plan.

The following Tuesday evening Jeremy had telephoned her to say that he was 'pissed off' and had been thinking about killing his family all day. She told him not to be so ridiculous and she said he made some response about tonight being the night. She claimed that he called her again at around 3 am to say that everything was going well and once more at around 6 am to inform her that Sheila had gone mad and that a police car would collect her and take her to Goldhanger.

Julie revealed that when she later asked Jeremy if he had killed his family he told her an elaborate story about hiring a hit man for £2,000. When Anthony Arlidge asked Julie why she had not reported this to the police she immediately replied: 'Jeremy said that if I ever said anything I could be implicated in the crime too because I knew about it. I was scared.'

Julie described a series of emotionally-charged rows she and Jeremy had endured over the following weeks. She was amazed by his lack of remorse for what he had done and became aware of a chasm slowly driving them apart. Jeremy admitted to Julie that he was unsure of his feelings for her, but she still loved him despite a growing dislike of the person he was becoming. The final straw in their relationship was when Jeremy rekindled his relationship with an old flame and flaunted it in front of Julie. The pair almost came to blows but Julie said Bamber restrained himself from hitting her when she threatened to report him to the police for the murders. Four days later, after much soul-searching and discussion with trusted friends, Julie Mugford decided to talk to the police.

Geoffrey Rivlin seized on Julie's status as the spurned woman to suggest that her statement to the police was made out of spite and jealousy. He suggested that she was envious of Bamber's relationship with his former girlfriend, Virginia Greaves, and that she had set her heart on marrying him. Julie was reduced to tears in the witness stand by Rivlin's relentless cross-examination: 'The reason I went to the police was that I couldn't cope with the guilt that I felt for Jeremy. That's the only reason I went to the police. Not because I felt he was slipping away from me, but because I couldn't cope with such a hideous thing.'

Rivlin decided it was time to unleash another blow to Julie Mugford's character. He asked her if she was honest and when she replied that she was he proceeded to tell the court that she had been involved in a burglary at the Osea Road Caravan Site. She had also been involved in a cheque book fraud with her friend, Susan Battersby.

Julie was unruffled and pointed out that she had later informed the bank manager and repaid the eight hundred pounds she had dishonestly obtained in goods by using fraudulent cheques. Rivlin reminded her that she had only contacted the bank after confessing to the police and receiving a caution.

Julie's ordeal was not over yet. Rivlin presented her with a pile of press cuttings and suggested that the information she had given in her statements to the police had, in fact, been gleaned from the media and not from Jeremy Bamber. Julie was insistent that all her knowledge of the shootings was based on what Jeremy had told her and that she had not bothered following the events in the newspapers.

Bloodstain expert John Hayward was able to tell the court that the stains on Sheila Caffell's nightdress indicated that she had been shot while she was in a reclining position but not while lying down. Her blood-soaked turquoise nightdress and Nevill's torn bloodied blue pyjama top were exhibited to the jury. Hayward revealed that when he had examined some of Jeremy Bamber's clothes several weeks after the murders, he had found spots of blood on them and also on the passenger seat of his car.

Regarding the blood on the silencer, Hayward testified

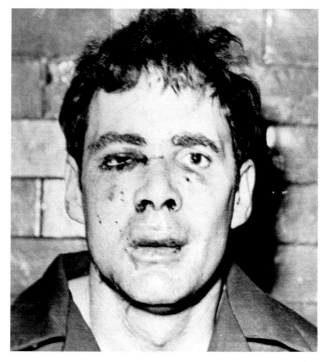

Donald Neilson bears the marks of his dramatic arrest – the black eye is the result of a punch thrown by a member of the public.

Lesley Whittle, a hard-working, home-loving teenager.

Donald Neilson and his wife Irene. In later years, Neilson forced his wife
and children to dress in combat gear and play soldiers.

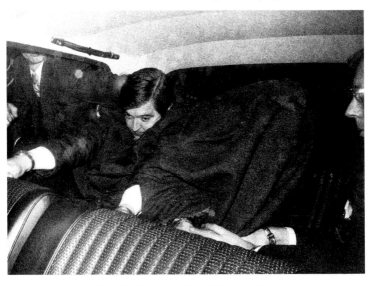

Prior to his conviction, Police had to go
to great lengths to protect Donald Neilson from an angry public.

'The face of evil.' Kenneth Noye following his arrest.

Flowers adorn the site where Stephen Cameron
died, and a newspaper poster shows just how
much publicity the case attracted.

Stephen Cameron, a happy young man with everything to live for.

Jeremy's sister Sheila, his mother June and Sheila's
twin sons Daniel and Nicholas.

Happy families. The Bamber family gather for Sheila's wedding. Jeremy, June
and Neville are on the left.

A cynical and calculated show of grief from Jeremy Bamber as he breaks down at the funeral. He is supported by his girlfriend of the time, Julie Mugford.

Finally the police have their man. A smirking Bamber is led away in handcuffs.

The beautiful farmhouse where Bamber murdered his family.

Leanne Tiernan (right) and her sister
Michelle. Leanne was only 16 when John
Taylor abducted her.

Although his neighbours thought he was
an 'ordinarly bloke', John Taylor's enjoyment
of torturing animals and his fascination with
sado-masochism was a precursor to murder.

that it belonged to Sheila but there was a very remote possibility that the blood inside the silencer could have been a mixture of June and Nevill Bamber's blood.

Home office pathologist Dr Peter Vanezis was next to take the witness stand. He described how Sheila had been blasted with two point blank gunshots to the neck: 'The first one was a flesh wound but the pain would have stunned her and if she had been left long enough she could have died from the bleeding. It is possible that the shock of the first injury caused her to involuntarily pull the trigger, releasing the shot to the base of the brain that killed her. However, Sheila's blood had been found on the silencer and if she had fired the first shot, she would have had to remove it, take it downstairs to the gun cupboard and return to the bedroom to shoot herself again.

'Considering the shock and pain she would have been in from the first blast that scenario is extremely unlikely. Forensics have also stated that Sheila would not have been able to reach the trigger with the silencer on so she could not have fired the shot.'

Bamber listened as Vanezis described how each family member had been slaughtered. He said that 61-year-old Nevill Bamber had suffered two black eyes and a fractured skull and that his body was covered in cuts and bruises. Vanezis said his injuries were consistent with a struggle to fight off his attacker. Seven bullets were pumped into Nevill Bamber and he was also bludgeoned with the rifle. Again, it seemed incredible to suggest that the strapping six foot four inches tall farmer had been overpowered by his slender daughter.

June Bamber had been shot seven times in the neck, arm and knee, twice in the chest, once between the eyes and once in the head. Vanezis believed June had tried to ward off the shots with her arms and legs and that was why she had received injuries to so many different parts of her body. The first five shots were administered while she was still in bed, but she had dragged herself to the doorway where she collapsed from a further two fatal shots to the head.

Venzis reported that the six-year-old twins, Nicholas and Daniel, had been killed by a hail of bullets that had been fired at point blank range to their heads, probably as they lay sleeping in their beds. Sheila Caffell had the two wounds beneath her chin but showed no signs of having attempted to defend herself against her attacker. Malcolm Fletcher, a ballistics officer from the Home Office forensic science laboratory in Huntingdon, reported on a series of tests he conducted with the .22 rifle. He conceded that there was a remote possibility that Sheila could have fired the shots herself if the silencer had been fitted, but female volunteers of a similar height found it physically impossible to press the trigger in controlled experiments.

He added that it was his opinion that the silencer had been fitted when both shots had been fired at Sheila Caffell and it was the action of the silencer being forced against flesh that caused the blood to seep into the silencer. He was also convinced that Sheila would probably have broken her nails while trying to reload the gun yet, 'Her nails were still in perfect condition and beautifully manicured.'

On the day of the killings, Jeremy Bamber had instructed the police to remove and destroy all the blood-stained mattresses, bedclothes and carpets at the house, consequently destroying potential evidence. Similarly, he insisted that his parents and sister be cremated, against June and Nevill's wishes. He reasoned that a burial would be inappropriate because their bodies weren't complete, but, in reality, a cremation prevented the bodies being excavated at a later date for further examination.

With the prosecution case complete, Jeremy Bamber took the stand. He denied killing his family and told the court that he had a loving relationship with his parents. He described his relationship with June as 'a standard loving, normal, caring relationship'. He admitted that on occasion they antagonised each other and that he had found Sheila hard to understand during the two years prior to her death. He said he found it difficult to cope with her claims that she was Joan of Arc or the Virgin Mary.

As the trial continued Jeremy Bamber became more evasive with his answers, despite the mounting evidence against him. The defence called a number of character witnesses. He was described as pleasant, charming, easy to deal with, polite, a hard worker and as someone who enjoyed a good relationship with his family. Things appeared to be looking up for Bamber. After days of character assassination he felt that the evidence was finally turning in his favour. The defence team also turned their attention to Sheila Caffell. Cross-examination of Dr Hugh Ferguson, the consultant psychiatrist who treated her at St Andrews Hospital, confirmed that Sheila used cannabis and cocaine despite warnings that it could lead to a relapse. He said she was prone to mood swings but he did not regard her as suicidal.

However, another consultant psychiatrist, Dr John Bradley, who was hired by the defence, had different ideas about Sheila. He said that Sheila's psychiatric history illustrated her obsession with evil and he had known cases where disturbed mothers would kill their family because they believed that was what was best for them.

In Rivlin's closing speech he told the jury that the case was lacking in proof and they should only convict Bamber if they were absolutely sure he was guilty. He added that there had not been any reliable forensic evidence to link Bamber with the murders and that the silencer evidence was unsatisfactory. He argued that Sheila Caffell was more than capable of carrying out the shootings when she was in the throes of one of her psychotic fits. As for the clean state of her body, he concluded that she may well have washed away the blood from the other bodies before shooting herself. And, as for the prosecution's number one witness, Julie Mugford, she was no more than an embittered, jilted lover.

In his summing up, the judge, Mr Justice Drake, asked the jury, 'Quite simply, do you believe Jeremy Bamber or do you believe Julie Mugford?'

After much deliberation the jury returned and announced that they had reached no unanimous verdict and needed more time. The judge sent the jurors to a hotel for the evening and Jeremy Bamber was sent to a cell beneath the courthouse. He was overheard discussing how much money he planned to sell his story to the newspapers for and was convinced that the jury would find him not guilty.

The following day, the jury returned to the court and the foreman announced that Bamber had been found guilty on five counts of murder. In each case the verdict had been reached by a majority of ten to two. Bamber swayed slightly in the dock as he attempted to absorb the news.

Sentencing Bamber to five sentences of life imprisonment, Mr Justice Drake said: 'Your conduct in planning and carrying out the killing of five members of your family was evil, almost beyond belief. It shows that you, young man that you are, have a warped and callous and evil mind behind an outwardly presentable and civilised appearance and manner.'

Bamber was led to the cell beneath the court to await the prison van and a long stretch behind bars.

Bamber has twice attempted and failed to have his case heard at the Court of Appeal. He renewed his application in the full Court of Appeal and in March 1989 his lawyer argued his case before the Lord Chief Justice of England, Lord Lane. Lord Lane sat with two other appeal judges, Mr Justice Roch and Mr Justice Henry. Rivlin argued that at Bamber's trial, Mr Justice Drake's summing up weighed heavily against Bamber by using forceful and extravagant language. The appeal judges rejected Geoffrey Rivlin's submissions and rejected

Bamber's leave to appeal. Lord Lane ruled that there was nothing unsatisfactory about the jury's verdicts and dismissed claims that the summing up was biased against Bamber and that the judge misdirected the jury.

Undeterred, Bamber continued to analyse with utmost scrutiny every statement, report and deposition of his case file to find inconsistencies that would give him grounds for appeal. Advances in medical science years later offered him his most promising breakthrough, because he could scientifically challenge the blood evidence on the silencer.

In 2002 Bamber was granted leave to appeal against his conviction. The main contention with his conviction was based on the blood evidence in the silencer. Hayward had conceded at the trial that there was a remote possibility that the blood grouping was the result of a mixture of June and Nevill Bamber's blood. Advances in DNA cast further doubt on the blood evidence. Forensics identified the DNA of at least two people inside the silencer and revealed that there was both male and female DNA present.

It wasn't possible to establish whose blood it was because, in 1996, Essex police destroyed all the blood exhibits in the Bamber case. After tracing Sheila's natural mother to obtain a sample of her DNA, it was established that the blood in the silencer did not belong to Sheila Caffell. Bamber claimed that the blood evidence had formed a crucial element of the prosecution case against him and he could now prove that it was incorrect.

The new evidence was not enough to free Bamber and his appeal was categorically rejected. The appeal judges ruled that despite questions about the blood, 'the totality of evidence' against Bamber remained overwhelming.

Jeremy Bamber is one of the few prisoners who have been told by the Home Secretary that he will never be released from prison. His life behind bars has been mixed. Shunned by many of his fellow inmates because of his upper class accent and educated background, Bamber busies himself by examining the finer details of his case. His conviction for one of the most heinous crimes of the last half century hasn't detracted from his magnetism to women. Fan mail still arrives for Bamber and he has had a string of glamorous girlfriends who have dutifully visited him in jail.

To this day, Bamber protests his innocence, maintaining that he was unfairly convicted on unreliable forensic evidence, but the judge, Sir Maurice Drake, remains convinced that the conviction was sound: 'Like the Court of Appeal and with some advantage over them because I sat through the trial and heard the witnesses first hand, I see nothing to suggest, even now with the advances in medical science, that the jury got the verdict wrong. A man who can kill the father and mother who have adopted him and given him a family ... then kill his sister and shoot her two six-year-old twins in bed, is evil beyond belief, surely.'

Ann Eaton and her family now live in White House Farm, but Ann remains haunted by Bamber: 'He should remain in prison for the rest of his life. Because if he is ever let out, heaven knows what would happen to the rest of my family. If he could kill his immediate family so easily ... we'd just be picked off one by one. We know that.'

3 A FACE FROM THE PAST: KENNETH NOYE

It was a fine spring day when Stephen Cameron encouraged his 17-year-old fiancée to drive his small red Rascal van. Danielle needed the practice and as it was a Sunday morning, Stephen thought the traffic would be light. The drive went well, and on their way home, Stephen diverted Danielle onto the M25 so they could go and buy some bagels in east London. It was the first time she had driven on a motorway and, even though it was Sunday lunchtime, the M25 was heavy with traffic.

Under Stephen's careful direction Danielle took the slip road for the M25 intersection with the M20, bringing her to the Swanley roundabout in Kent, which is one of the busiest traffic islands in Europe. Cautiously she manoeuvred around the island but in a moment's confusion she made a late lane change, inadvertently cutting in front of a Land Rover Discovery. As she approached the next set of traffic lights she hit her brakes hard. The Land Rover pulled sharply in front of her and braked abruptly, halting without warning. The male driver stepped out of the vehicle and strode purposefully towards their red van. 'Stay here,' Stephen cautioned Danielle as he opened the passenger door to climb out and meet the other motorist.

Lorry driver, Jon Saunders, was approaching the same intersection at 1.20 pm on that May 19 afternoon in 1996. He used the road every day and was familiar with the phasing system on the traffic lights. He willed the first set of lights to be on green, because he knew then he would probably make it through the next few sets without stopping.

He says, 'I sailed through the first few sets without braking, and as I approached another set, which looked like they were about to turn green, I could see there were several vehicles queuing in the nearside lane. Two men climbed out of the front couple of vehicles and started talking. I thought maybe they were discussing directions.

'Suddenly their body language deteriorated and it escalated into a fight. They were punching and kicking each other, spinning around into the road. I couldn't believe what I was seeing and tried to use the size of my vehicle to bring them to their senses. I moved closer and started to hoot my horn, but they were oblivious. The lights changed, and as I moved through them I kept my eyes fixed on the two men in my rear view mirror. They were still knocking seven bells out of each other, so I pulled clear of the junction and called the police on my mobile phone.'

Frozen with fear, Danielle sat in the van and watched the savage confrontation in helpless horror. Her mind was racing as she desperately tried to think of a way to halt the fracas. Other vehicles whirled around the stationary van, some angrily hooting their horns in protest at the obstruction, others staring with morbid curiosity, but unwilling to stop and help. Finally, the vicious struggle ceased and, as the driver of the Land Rover returned to his vehicle, Danielle forced herself to stagger to the aid of her beaten fiancé, who was stumbling in the road. As she hesitantly stepped forward, the Land Rover driver turned on his heel in an instant and was once again hurtling towards them, his face contorted with anger.

He was clutching something metallic that glinted in the sunlight; Danielle realised that it was a knife. Terror gripped her. She pleaded with him not to hurt Stephen, but feared that if she moved any closer he would lash out at her too.

Danielle screamed as the Land Rover driver punched the knife into Stephen's chest, piercing his heart and liver with the razor-sharp, nine-inch blade. With her cries still ringing in the air, the Land Rover driver strode confidently back to his vehicle and wove between the lanes of traffic to disappear without trace.

Jon Saunders watched in disbelief as Stephen slumped to the ground. Jumping out of his lorry he dashed to help the injured man. Danielle was screaming hysterically, cradling Stephen in her arms and pleading with him: 'Don't leave me, Stephen. Don't go.' Her body heaved with the intensity of her sobs, her tears diluting the blood that gushed from his severely injured thorax.

By now another woman had got out of her car to help. She urged Jon to call an ambulance while she worked futilely to stem the heavy flow oozing out of Stephen's wounds. His eyes were rolling, his consciousness ebbing away as he slipped towards death. An hour later Stephen Cameron was pronounced dead.

Danielle later tearfully told a news conference: 'Stephen said, "He stabbed me, Dan. Get his number plate," and I called the number plate out to him. I went and held him and he just looked at me as if to say, please help me, and there was nothing I could do.'

Several miles away in Norfolk, Det Supt Nick Biddiss was playing golf with his colleagues. His game was interrupted by a telephone call from a journalist enquiring about a fatal stabbing on the M25. Unaware of the tragic killing, Det Supt Biddiss switched on the television news and absorbed the scanty preliminary details that the press were able to divulge. Several days later Nick Biddiss was to be appointed to lead the international hunt for Stephen Cameron's killer – the man who would become dubbed the Road Rage Killer.

Scenes of crime officers mounted a fingertip search of the crime scene, but there was nothing to identify the killer. The only DNA sample available was possible from the pools of blood saturating the road, and tests revealed that it belonged to the victim. There was no sign of any murder weapon either. Information flooded into the incident room from passing motorists, but much of it was conflicting. Det Supt Biddiss diligently assessed the statements of 29 witnesses who were driving by at the time.

He explains, 'There were plenty of witnesses coming forward, and we hoped somebody would be able to give us the registration number of the vehicle. In theory you would have thought that with so many witnesses about on such a busy road, it would have been fairly straightforward to trace the driver. Unfortunately, everybody thought somebody else had noted down the registration details, so the best that we ended up with was that it was an L-registered Land Rover Discovery.

'Some witnesses described the vehicle as maroon; one said it was green, others a blue one, a grey one and even black. In the sunlight these metallic paint effects can look very different, so we couldn't be exactly sure what colour it was. Then we had an added problem because there were 17,000 Land Rover Discoveries registered in the country with the combination of letters we had ascertained from witnesses. It was like looking for a needle in a haystack.'

Jon Saunders was visited at home by the police to see if he could help them piece together the sequence of events. He told the investigating officers: 'I tried to get a good look at the man. As he drove away he sort of looked back and sneered at me. He had dark hair and looked as if he was in his mid-forties and fairly well-heeled. I am fairly sure that the Land Rover Discovery was dark blue and I can confirm that it was L-registered.'

Descriptions of the suspect at this stage provided nothing substantial to act on, and Nick Biddiss knew that the vehicle was his best lead. By now the police had pieced together five of the seven letters and numbers from witness reports. 'I was confident that we would find the person responsible for killing Stephen Cameron, but I knew that as time went on it would become more likely that the Land Rover Discovery, which was a key part of our evidence, would get sold on or disposed of.'

The police trawled through long hours of videotapes recorded by surveillance cameras positioned alongside the motorway, desperately hoping to catch a fleeting glimpse of the Land Rover. They were gravely disappointed to discover that the vital camera on the Swanley intersection was not set up to record on the day of the murder, so there was no footage of the incident or of the approaching vehicles.

Biddiss instructed his team to run the registration plate details through the Police National Computer and to look for matching vehicles registered to addresses in a ten-mile radius of the crime scene. There were many cars listed which approximated the incomplete number plate they had. One of these was a Land Rover Discovery with the registration mark L794 JTF, which was listed at an address in Bridgen Road, Bexley, exactly ten miles from the scene of the murder. The owner was Anthony Francis.

The nation was mesmerised by the callous road rage confrontation that had ended in murder. Every national newspaper carried the story on the front page. Gary Jones, a reporter for *The News of the World*, was assigned to follow the story. 'It was just a very unusual crime. Most murders take place one on one, away from public view. But for someone to be stabbed so openly on a Sunday afternoon on one of the busiest roads in Europe was staggering. Road rage was the new buzz-word in Britain. People were fascinated by the fact that you could lose your life by getting into an altercation with a complete stranger while out driving.

'We'd heard that things like this happened in America, where people would get shot for no apparent reason, but no one quite believed it could happen in Britain. Most people have encountered an angry motorist; suddenly they realised that next time it could be them who got killed. It was a scary thought to carry around with you.'

Four days after the murder, the police appeared on the television programme *Crimewatch* to appeal for further information and for witnesses to come forward. The appeal was a success and new leads poured into the incident room, but Nick Biddiss felt it was an ill-timed plea for help. 'We should have waited for a month before we went on *Crimewatch*. We were already overwhelmed by the intelligence pouring in, and *Crimewatch* prompted even more telephone calls and paperwork, not all of it useful.

'Although people were genuinely trying to help, we were given a lot of misleading information which we had to spend vital time following up in order to rule it out. People would call in and say things like, "I know some-body from the north of Scotland who owns a Land Rover Discovery and he looks like your photo fit." So we would send detectives to follow that up and it would be a dead end. I'm not saying people shouldn't phone in with this kind of information. It's just that we didn't time the appeal properly and we ended up chasing a lot of false leads when we could have been applying our energies in a more useful direction.'

Biddiss carefully scrutinised the most promising leads the police had acquired and was intrigued by Anthony Francis. He decided to focus his attention and the efforts of his officers on pursuing this line of inquiry. He informed his team that finding Francis was a priority. Several miles away, Flying Squad Officer Anthony Brightwell stopped in his tracks when he heard who Kent Police were looking for. 'I was totally shocked when I heard the name Anthony Francis, because I immediately recognised it as an alias for Kenneth Noye.' Noye was a high-profile and notorious criminal whose wealth and illegal activities had occupied numerous headlines in the early 1980s. The police investigation had led them to a man who embraced crime as a profession and as a result had accumulated staggering riches and power.

Kenneth Noye was born on May 14 1947 in Bexleyheath. He was the son of GPO engineer, James Noye, and his wife, Edith, who worked three days a week at the Crayford Dog Track. Mrs Noye could never think ill of her beloved son, even when, as a child, he was caught stealing money from the till of a department store. At the age of 11, Kenneth started attending Bexleyheath Secondary Modern School, where fellow pupils later accused him of running a protection racket. As a teenager he served a year's sentence in a borstal for receiving stolen cars, and as an adult he slipped seamlessly between the criminal underworld and the company of police officers and socialites. Those in his company were bedazzled by him. He commanded respect and enjoyed a luxurious lifestyle that was a far cry from his working-class upbringing.

Noye's wife, Brenda, a legal secretary, quickly fell under his captivating spell. They met while Noye was waiting in legal chambers for a charge against him to be heard in court. The unlikely couple married in 1970 and had two sons, Kevin and Brett. Noye and his family lived at Hollywood Cottage in Kent. When the existing cottage burned down, Kenneth Noye commissioned an extravagant palatial new property set in the sprawling 15 acres of land. By the early 1970s, Noye was already on the fringes of serious crime. He would regularly socialise at the Hilltop Hotel near his home, where the gangster elite – the Krays, the Richardsons, the Haywards and Frankie Fraser – would drink Dom Perignon while watching the cabaret.

Noye earned himself a reputation as a reliable fence who could shift anything and as an armourer who could supply guns. He also developed a keen interest in the gold smuggling trade, and between 1982 and 1984 he ran smuggling operations worth a staggering £35 million. His own cut amounted to just under £4.5 million, but Noye was always on the lookout for more. Despite his quickly accumulating wealth, he couldn't resist getting something for nothing and was convicted in 1979 for illegally extracting electricity from his house.

Noye also had the vision and the means to infiltrate legitimate business and made much of his money through seemingly legal enterprises – property development, transport and various financial operations. He was a successful businessman with an impressive network of contacts, but the police were curious about how lawful some of his transactions were.

Kent Police soon confirmed that Anthony Francis and Kenneth Noye were the same person. They obtained mortgage documents in the name of Anthony Francis and matched fingerprints from them to prints from Kenneth Noye previously stored in the national police records. The problem was Kenneth Noye had gone missing without trace.

Having made his statement, witness Jon Saunders was eager to put the experience of May 19 behind him. 'I never bought any of the newspapers. I tried to put the whole thing to the back of my mind and get on with my life. There was a lot of gossip locally. People said they had seen Kenneth Noye at the golf course, in a restaurant and all kinds of places. I thought it was far-fetched.

'I felt that this guy knew he was in trouble and had fled. I didn't think he would come back where he knew that the police could find him. The man had a reputation, but I didn't think he would be foolish enough to try to interfere with witnesses.'

Kent Police first came into contact with Noye when they suspected his involvement in one of the largest gold bullion robberies ever seen in Britain. In 1983, six masked raiders forced their way into the top-security Brink Mats depot beneath the Heathrow flight path. Three of them were armed with revolvers and automatic pistols. It was 6.30 am on a cold Saturday in November and the security guards had just started their shift when the armed raiders, disguised as security personnel, burst into the building. They successfully disabled a huge array of electronic security devices, enabling them to enter the heart of the depot. Quickly and viciously they overpowered the guards, striking one savagely with a gun on the back of the head. They forced the terrified security officers to kneel on the floor while cloth bags were pulled roughly over their heads. They poured petrol over two of them from the waist down and threatened to set them alight if they didn't co-operate.

The masked men grabbed two of the blindfolded security officers and dragged them down the stairs and through the security gates to the vaults. These contained consignments of currency, diamonds and precious metals ready to be shipped all around the world. Each security officer knew only half of the combination number for the safe where the vast sums of cash were also stored. 'Open them up!' the robbers ordered. One of the shaking men reluctantly muttered his half of the combination code. They turned expectantly to the other guard, but he was shuddering violently, his body and brain so possessed by abject terror that he couldn't even remember his own name. Fearing he was about to be set alight, he tried to recall telephone numbers, bank account numbers, anything that would help him retrieve the crucial combination. But his memory betrayed him.

The armed raiders exploded into a fury, threatening to set him alight in an instant if he didn't recall the code.

They paced impatiently outside the vaults, bellowing at the guard that his time was running out. As the seconds ticked away one of the masked thieves suddenly noticed that there were pallets piled high just outside the door. He walked over to them to take a cursory glance inside. They were overflowing with gold bullion, destined for a Cathay Pacific flight to Hong Kong later that morning, where they would be traded on the market.

The raiders realised that this was potentially a far greater prize than their intended £3 million cash haul. Using the warehouse's own forklift trucks, they transported the 76 boxes of gold into a waiting van. Despite the weight of the bullion, it took just five minutes to load the 2,670 kilos of gold bars, worth over £26 million, and make their getaway. They also escaped with £100,000 worth of cut and uncut diamonds. Anthony Brightwell, a Detective Inspector with the Flying Squad, was the first police officer to arrive on the scene.

'It was total disarray. The area where the guards had been attacked had chairs thrown and overturned all over the place. We found handcuffs and ropes, and there was a pungent smell of petrol permeating the air. The scene instantly suggested there had been a violent armed robbery.

'Two of the security officers required medical attention, and of course they had to change clothes to remove the petrol they had been doused in. This was a watershed crime, as never before had that amount of gold bullion been stolen in one swoop. The robbery had been carried out with military precision and executed like a military assault. It appeared to be the work of a highly professional team.'

The police quickly established that there were links between the Brinks Mat heist and another robbery at Security Express earlier that year, in which £6 million in used currency was stolen. Just as in the Brinks Mat raid, armed masked robbers had burst into the warehouse and poured petrol over the guards, threatening to set them alight if they didn't co-operate. The police felt that both robberies had involved employees of each company because of the easy access the robbers had gained and their precise knowledge of how security procedures operated.

Armed robbery was prolific in the 1980s, but it was mostly security vans and banks that were targeted. The Security Express and Brinks Mat robberies appeared to be the work of an organised crime gang who had spent months planning the large-scale operations.

Gold bars such as those stolen from Brinks Mat are all easily identifiable by a refiner's stamp. These special markings are intended to ensure that the gold will be a liability to dispose of. The market is fairly small, and Brinks Mat and Engleharts, who lost the bullion, are two of the main gold dealers in the world. The likelihood was that the thieves would offer them their own smelted gold back for purchase.

The Flying Squad established a connection between Brinks Mat security guard Anthony Black, who was on duty at the time of the robbery, and another man, Brian Robinson, known in criminal circles as the Colonel.

Brian Robinson's common law wife was Anthony Black's sister, and once the link was established the police turned their attention to the relationship between the two men.

Investigating detectives were also suspicious about the fact that Black had turned up late for work on that fateful morning. Did he know that something was about to happen? During a police video reconstruction of the raid, Black claimed that he had left a jacket hanging over a chair and that his diary was inside it. Unbeknown to Black, the diary – a blank one – had been photocopied by the police.

A week later, when the police formally interviewed Black, he produced the diary, which now had backdated appointments on the previously blank pages. Officers believed he was trying to cover his tracks. The appointments coincided with when the police suspected he had been meeting with the criminal gang to plan the robbery. It was an inside job. Black confessed his involvement to the police and implicated three other people as part of the gang.

The police estimated that 15 people were involved in planning the Brinks Mat robbery, but only four men were eventually convicted, and much of the gold has never been recovered.

Robinson's partner in crime was Mickey McAvoy, considered by the police to be one of south London's most prolific armed robbers. Prior to the Brinks Mat robbery, both were living in modest council houses, but just a few weeks after the heist they purchased substantial homes in Kent, both paid for in cash. Rumours also abounded that McAvoy had bought two Rottweilers to protect his new mansion and unsubtly named them Brinks and Mat.

Police discovered that the Brinks Mat gang had sought the assistance of a criminal known as Fox, who arranged for the gold to be delivered to a variety of locations where it could be smelted down into a more manageable form. One of Mickey McAvoy's associates, Brian Perry, introduced Kenneth Noye to the gang, and he offered his assistance and expertise in the gold smelting trade.

Everything seemed to be falling into place, but the gang made a fatal mistake when they attempted to spend their laundered cash. They continually withdrew large amounts of the laundered money from a single branch of a bank in Bristol. The amounts were so phenomenal that the bank was forced to request additional funds from the Bank of England. This attracted attention from the Treasury and, unsurprisingly, the police. Kenneth Noye, amongst others, was placed under surveillance.

In June 1984, the year following the Brinks Mat raid, an alert policeman noticed Kenneth Noye purchasing eleven gold bars from Charter House Jaffe Bank in Jersey. Subsequent police enquiries revealed that Noye had arrived at the bank with no appointment and produced a bag containing £50,000 in £50 notes. Their suspicions aroused, they kept him under surveillance for the remainder of his trip. Noye left the gold bars with a safe deposit box company in Jersey and returned to London.

The police discovered that Noye was closely associated with suspects they had charged in connection with the Brinks Mat robbery and surmised that he was the courier the robbers were using to dispose of the gold bullion. They believed his gold purchase in Jersey was to secure documentation and receipts that would enable him to move eleven bars of Brinks Mat gold around the country and dispose of them without attracting unwelcome attention.

Flying Squad Officer Anthony Brightwell, at the centre of the investigation into Noye, could understand only too well why he would be the gang's choice to assist with the disposal. 'He was a wheeler dealer at that time. A guy who was involved in fencing lorry loads, fencing goods, placing them and organising their disposal. He was well-connected and cunning. This kind of operation required a great deal of cunning and subtlety to pull it off. Noye had a reputation for being a man who possessed these traits.'

Noye's close association with high-ranking criminals was well-known to the police, but until the gold bullion connection they had viewed him mostly as a small-time criminal. His most recent conviction had been in 1981, for smuggling a Magnum handgun in parts through the postal system from America. He didn't appear to be in the forefront of serious crime, but they were acutely aware that he was an active background player.

Anthony Brightwell recalls: 'The first thing we did

was to look at his lifestyle. His house, Hollywood Cottage, barely describes the place we found. Rather than a small cottage, it was a considerable property protected by electronic gates, with a driveway that was at least a hundred yards from the gates to the door. It had an indoor swimming pool in a Roman-style setting, and it was clear that this man was extremely wealthy. The style of the house was rather like a film set. It was showy, with lots of onyx and gilt. It had a Roman Empire look, and there were the most expensive fittings I've ever seen. I thought it was rather gaudy and over the top. It wasn't to my taste at all.'

Although Kenneth Noye enjoyed opulent surroundings at home, he refrained from self-aggrandisement away from it, opting for Land Rovers instead of Ferraris and shunning the yachting lifestyle or anything people would consider too flash for a supposedly averagely successful businessman. Unlike the Krays, who were famously photographed by David Bailey, Noye eschewed publicity. His cousin Michael Noye once told the press: 'Kenny didn't like any photos of himself floating around. He knew that if people outside his own circle didn't know what he looked like, then he would be able to move around much more easily.'

The police decided that Kenneth Noye was worth closer scrutiny and arranged for a set of aerial photographs to be taken of his home. The house was built on an old Second World War fighter aerodrome, and the grounds contained old underground war bunkers and large stores that could provide the perfect hiding place for stolen goods. Officers appointed to keep the house under surveillance noticed that Noye was spending an unusual amount of time with a man called Brian Reader. In the early 1980s Reader had fled abroad, while on trial for burglary. He assumed a false name and identity and later returned to England. The police followed Reader to an after-office-hours meeting with several businessmen who worked for a bullion company in London and observed him handing over a heavily laden bag. The undercover officers continued to trail Reader and Noye and witnessed further meetings at Noye's house or in lay-bys and car parks between London and Kent. They were convinced that they were watching the disposal of gold bullion stolen from Brinks Mat.

To confirm their suspicions the police needed to get closer to Noye and his property, but they were wary of alerting him before they had secured their evidence. To ensure their investigations remained covert they called in SAS-trained rural surveillance officers Neil Murphy and John Fordham. It was a fateful decision that would tear the investigation apart.

Murphy and Fordham surveyed the property. It was full of nooks and crannies where the gold could easily be stashed. Murphy knew they would have a limited chance to fulfil their brief. 'Our instructions were to observe a hand-over and try to establish where the gold was being stored. We weren't certain if Reader was bringing the gold to Noye or if Noye was handing the gold over to Reader, but one thing was for sure: Reader was making almost daily visits.'

The surveillance officers studied the aerial photographs of Hollywood Cottage and established that the woodland surrounding the house would provide reasonable cover for them to hide in. To achieve a successful result they would have to conduct the whole procedure without attracting any attention from Noye or his associates. 'The Metropolitan Police had noticed that a number of criminals had recently bought large houses in Kent and Essex. They were smart crooks and had purchased properties in places that were difficult to watch without being seen. To try and tackle this problem we approached the army to develop a course to train us in SAS-style surveillance and survival techniques. Once trained, we were known as rural surveillance officers. Our main concern with Noye's property was to make sure we didn't arouse the attention of his three Rottweilers. 'We'd done jobs in the past with dogs and you never know how they are going to react. Most of the time if you stay still the dog will get bored and go away, but it's not an exact science,' says Murphy.

The two officers reported for duty at 6 pm and were preparing to work a 12-hour shift. It was winter, so they were clothed warmly in balaclava hats and thick camouflage jackets to protect them from the early morning December frosts. 'We were expecting it to be a pretty boring shift, but within minutes of us being there Reader showed up. It was action time.'

Murphy and Fordham signalled to the control officers that Reader was approaching the property and they were given orders to get as close to the house as possible and observe what they could through any cracks in the curtains or open windows. They clambered quietly over the wall and, using the soft reflected light from the house to see by, they crept stealthily through the trees up to the side of the building. The dead leaves and sticks crunched beneath their feet, while the dense woodland crowded around them, throwing threatening shadowy obstacles in their path.

Suddenly both men jumped. They could hear the brusque barking of Noye's dogs, and the ferocious sound was drawing rapidly closer. Soon it was within feet of them. Murphy knew that the relentless barking would alarm Noye and bring him to investigate. He signalled to Fordham that it was time to exit the property.

'The Rottweilers were jumping up at us, barking like mad and making a racket. I gave John the nod to say, "let's go." It was very dark and I just assumed he was following me. Then I heard voices and, realising John was at risk of being discovered, I pretended to be a neighbour and shouted: "Can someone shut those dogs up!" I hoped they would quieten the dogs to avoid upsetting the neighbours, but it was no good. John had already been rumbled.'

Keeping close to the ground, Murphy gradually crawled to safety at the front perimeter of the property and alerted his colleagues that Fordham required back-up urgently. Peering back through the main gates, he could see Noye and Reader leaning over John, who was huddled on the ground. 'I saw Mrs Noye join the group and then walk away again. Then I heard Noye shouting at John to show them his ID. I heard more talking and then Noye bellowed, "I'll blow your head off," and I panicked because I thought he'd got a gun and I knew John wasn't armed.

'The firing squad burst in and within seconds arrested Noye. Reader fled towards the house but was apprehended by the Flying Squad as he attempted to escape from the rear of the property. John was discovered prostrate on the cold, hard earth and, as officers moved closer to lift him to safety, he gasped: 'He's done me. He's stabbed me.' Fordham had been brutally knifed ten times.

Anthony Brightwell was sitting in the control room at Scotland Yard monitoring events. 'Everyone was full of great expectancy that night. We thought we were on the verge of cracking a big case and finding out where the gold was coming from. All of a sudden all hell broke loose and it quickly became apparent that the evening had turned into a total disaster.'

Officer Murphy accompanied his wounded colleague in the ambulance, relieved to see John's chest still moving. He commented to the paramedic that it was a good sign that John was still breathing, still fighting for his life. 'He's not breathing,' the paramedic replied gently. 'That's the oxygen I'm giving him that's pushing his lungs out. He's in a bad way.' Murphy paced the hospital corridor waiting for news of his severely injured colleague. Hours later the news came. Officer Fordham – who was married with two children – had failed to survive the pernicious stabbing inflicted on him by Kenneth Noye.

Murphy was devastated: 'I couldn't believe what had happened. Working with John was such a treat. He was the best in the business and other officers were even jealous that I was working with the top guy every day. He had great experience and I was forever learning something new from him. He was always trying to find news ways to improve the way we were working.

'I honestly thought he was following me out of the woods that night. I didn't realise until it was too late that he was still in position. I can only guess that he had decided to stay perfectly still to try to shake off the dogs. Unfortunately, Noye came out and discovered him before the dogs lost interest.'

Kenneth Noye was charged with murder. Flying Squad Officer Anthony Brightwell interviewed him at Dartford Police Station in Kent. 'Myself and two colleagues from the Flying Squad interviewed Noye three days after the killing. As soon as I walked into the interview room he came towards me to shake my hand, and I immediately recognised it as the handshake of a Freemason. I believe he did this in order to curry favour with me in the hope that I was a fellow mason and would help him.'

Noye had joined the Hammersmith Freemasons Lodge in west London back in 1977. He was proposed and seconded by two police officers and frequently rubbed shoulders with officers of the law, who occasionally helped him to sidestep detection and prosecution. He hoped that such common ground would help him to evade prosecution for killing John Fordham.

Brightwell wasn't prepared to negotiate. 'I could tell from his mannerisms that here was a man who was used to getting his own way. He was manipulative and was looking for angles and help. Throughout the interview he was continually searching for assistance in a situation where he was beyond help.

'My response was that he had killed a police officer and that left no room for manoeuvre. For us to be seen cutting deals with someone who had killed a fellow officer was taboo. It was out of the question. He was on his own. He was going to stand trial for murder.

'Not only did we lose a loyal and particularly well-liked police officer, but following his death the investigation also collapsed and the chances of us ever recovering all the gold bullion dissipated. It was a total disaster.'

The investigation into the gold bullion disposal paled into the background beside the fact that a police officer had been fatally stabbed while carrying out his duties. The odds looked stacked against Noye, but his defence counsel, John Matthews, one of the country's leading barristers at the time, felt that his client could make a strong argument for having acted in self-defence.

'People thought it was a clear-cut case. You hear that somebody attacks an unarmed police officer, stabbing him ten times with a knife, and when you string those facts together the general perception is that there can't be any justification for that.

'When the victim is a police officer, the defendant starts with a distinct psychological disadvantage in front of a jury. It is difficult to work against that. However, when I read the prosecution evidence and the initial statement from Kenneth Noye, my first reaction was that he did have a very good defence.'

Noye relayed to the jury how he was alarmed and concerned by the dogs barking and cautiously ventured out to investigate what had disturbed them. He went to his car to grab a torch, and while he was there he picked up a kitchen knife that he had been using earlier that day to clean out the battery terminal. He walked warily into the woodland shouting: 'Who's there?' and was shocked to stumble across a man wearing a balaclava and camouflage suit. He told the court that he had acted in self-defence, that Fordham had struck him and lurched on top of him. Noye insisted that he only stabbed John Fordham because he believed without any doubt that his own life was at risk.

He told the court that, 'The whole thing was so frightening. I thought I was being killed. I didn't think I had a chance of living. I was fighting for my life. I was just in a total panic. This man was on top of me and I was stabbing away with this knife in a frenzy.' His explanation corroborated evidence of the various positions of the stab wounds and why they were so fatally deep.

Noye's defence counsel advised the jury that, 'The police had no right to send in an officer dressed like that with no formal identification. Noye didn't know who he was. As far as he was concerned, he was confronted with a masked stranger that he had found trespassing in his grounds. He was entitled to defend himself. The fact that there were ten stab wounds in different parts of the body just corroborates Noye's insistence that he'd struck out in fear.'

The barrister applied to the judge to take the jury, under police guard, to Noye's garden, late at night, so that they could experience first hand the fear the defendant had faced that evening. It was a master-stroke on behalf of the defence. John Matthews was delighted when the judge agreed. 'It was very effective from the jury's point of view. They were kept segregated and weren't allowed to ask questions. When we went down there it was a dark, blustery night with a slither of moon shining through the woods. It was really quite scary, and I think it had a great deal of effect on the jury. They understood how Noye must have felt, all on his own, shining his torch onto a man who is lurking in his woods. They could understand why he retaliated as he did and they reflected this in their verdict.'

It took the jury of seven men and five women, 12½ hours to reach their verdict of not guilty. Kenneth Noye was acquitted. When he and Brian Reader heard the verdict they shouted to the jury, 'God bless you all.' Noye added, 'That's what I am, not guilty.'

Noye walked free from court to celebrate the verdict, but his barrister faced a bewildered public. 'The man on the street was absolutely amazed by the verdict. They felt it was a travesty, but of course they hadn't heard the evidence. They hadn't been to Hollywood Cottage to experience the conditions that Noye faced. They hadn't heard Noye in the witness box. People would say to me it was an amazing result, but I would reply that it was always on the cards and that it was the right result.'

Neil Murphy was saddened by the verdict but comforted himself that his colleague's killer would probably pay the price for the stabbing at a later date. 'Police officers have a phrase that goes, "They will come again." It means that if someone walks away from court when we feel they are guilty, then we expect them to re-offend and they will be convicted the next time. So justice usually works its way through in the end.'

He was right. Kenneth Noye walked free from court after killing John Fordham, but he still had to face charges regarding the gold bullion. A police search of his property following the stabbing of John Fordham uncovered 11 bars of gold. The police also discovered copper coins used in smelting and, bizarrely, a copy of *The Guinness Book of Records* with the Brinks Mat robbery entry circled.

Noye vehemently denied handling the stolen Brinks Mat gold but admitted that he was operating a VAT fraud. He confessed he was buying gold abroad without paying VAT on it and then selling it on to the legitimate market in the UK, charging the value added tax but deliberately withholding the money from the tax office. Despite his protestations, he was convicted of conspiracy to handle the stolen gold and of various VAT-evasion charges. He was fined £700,000 and handed a 14-year prison sentence.

When he heard the verdict, Noye's legitimate businessman's mask slipped for the first time as he turned to the jury in a bitter rage and spat at them: 'I hope you all die of cancer.'

Noye served eight years of his jail term, but his life was turned upside down by the investigation. He was declared bankrupt and was forced to sell his beloved Hollywood Cottage.

However, his notoriety served him well. While in Albany prison on the Isle Of Wight he secured a comfortable position as a gym orderly and settled into prison life. An officer who worked at another jail where Noye was detained was taken aback by his popularity. 'He was highly respected and well-liked amongst the prisoners and the staff. A lot of the prisoners don't like the police, so they admired him for killing a serving officer. It greatly enhanced his reputation in jail.

'At that time [the prison] was one of the worst places a prisoner could be sent because there were a lot of violent assaults. Kenny never had any problems though. The other prisoners were looking to do him favours. They would do anything to befriend a well-known inmate.'

In 1996, when Stephen Cameron was murdered, the police had heard little of significance about Kenneth Noye since his release from prison in 1994. He spent his first month out of jail in Northern Cyprus, where he is believed to have met and befriended Asil Nadir, the former boss of Polly Peck. They allegedly discussed business opportunities to exploit the area's growing tourist trade and Noye was persuaded to invest in a timeshare development.

Noye quickly rebuilt his network of contacts and re-established his flourishing financial empire. He was back on the circuit and managed to avoid the attention of the police until he became a suspect in the case of Stephen Cameron's murder.

Once the link was confirmed between the names Anthony Francis and Kenneth Noye, the police placed Noye high on their list of suspects. But before they could interview him, they needed to trace him. Det Supt Biddiss deployed officers to check out Anthony Francis's address and, as he suspected, neither the Land Rover Discovery nor Kenneth Noye were at home.

'His wife, Brenda, ran a squash club in Dartford, and when we made enquiries there, we were quickly turned away. We went into pubs and places we knew that Noye frequented and questioned people he associated with, but they kept telling us that Noye wasn't around. Then we started getting solicitors' letters telling us that if we wanted to speak to these people then we must do it through a lawyer. We felt this was an odd reaction if they had nothing to hide. We were suspicious of their secrecy.

'On paper Noye was bankrupt. He didn't have any money so he couldn't have a bank account, credit cards or anything that showed he had property. This was probably one reason why he used false names, so that he could own properties and develop business interests without arousing any unwelcome attention. I believe he had access to money that would be beyond the dreams of a lottery winner. He lived the lifestyle of someone wealthy and high-profile, and yet on paper he had nothing.

'We made a complete forensic search of his house and we discovered a new Land Rover Discovery in the drive that Kenny had purchased the day after the murder, paid for with £12,000 in cash, handed over in a carrier bag. I believe he planted it there as a decoy car to mislead us. We had another tip-off that he had taken the Land Rover Discovery that we suspected had been used in the murder to a scrapyard. We were told it had been taken there the night after the incident. Unfortunately, we were unable to find anything conclusive at the scrapyard.'

However, further enquiries revealed that Noye had been in the right place at the right time when the stabbing took place. Police traced the positions of the calls made on his mobile phone on the day of the murder and were able to plot his journey in detail. Data from the mobile phone masts and beacons situated along the M25 confirmed that he had been making calls that firmly placed him in the vicinity around the time of the of the killing. Det Supt Biddiss was finally able to gather some concrete evidence that placed Noye in the frame for having committed the crime. 'I imagine he was in a total panic and he's making all these calls on his mobile phone with no thought of how they could be traced in the future.'

Biddiss was also deeply suspicious of Noye's sudden disappearance. 'He was a person who, despite his criminal history, was quite high-profile in the west Kent area. He socialised a lot, he was well-known and an active member of the community. To disappear like he did was out of character. He missed several appointments and nobody appeared to know where he was.

'Of course, when you start asking questions there's always a risk that your enquiries may eventually feed through the grapevine back to Kenny Noye, but we did all we could to keep it as low-profile as possible.'

But while Nick Biddiss was making painstaking moves to ensure that the police pursuit of Noye remained under wraps, the media were poised to blow their cover right out of the water. 'I got a call from *The Mirror*, who had received a tip-off that we wanted to speak to Kenneth Noye. I informed the reporter that it wasn't my policy to discuss who we were looking for, but he said that they had reliable sources and were going to run it as a main story. This would have seriously compromised our investigation so I invited him to meet me to discuss the implications. I laid my cards firmly on the table, and after further talks with his editor they agreed to pull the story for the time being.'

But unbeknown to Biddiss *The News of the World* was also in receipt of a tip-off. Reporter Ian Edmundson received an excited call: 'I was contacted by a well-respected informant who I had discussed crime stories with for years. He sounded very nervous and said he had something big to tell me but he didn't want to discuss it over the telephone. We arranged to meet at a pub near Greenwich. Over a few drinks he told me that the police thought Kenneth Noye had killed Stephen Cameron. My jaw just hit the floor. I thought there must be more to it than road rage because I couldn't imagine Kenny Noye losing his rag over a traffic incident and risking going back to prison.

'I went straight to the office and remember standing there with the picture editor and the news editor comparing library shots of Kenneth Noye with the police photo fit. The two were identical. It was uncanny.'

Det Supt Nick Biddiss was dismayed by the news that another national newspaper had picked up the trail. 'I got a call from *The News of the World* on the Friday and my fears were aroused immediately. I know that when a Sunday paper calls on a Friday they are chasing quotes for a story they are going to print that weekend. As I suspected, they too had received a tip-off that we wanted to talk to Kenneth Noye in relation to Stephen Cameron's murder.

'I explained the sensitivity of the information and asked them not to run the story, but they went ahead and 36 hours later it was splashed in that weekend's edition. I was absolutely livid because identification of the suspect was a key factor in this investigation and yet they printed both the story and a photograph of Noye. It was irresponsible journalism. Now we were in a position where Kenneth Noye's defence lawyers could claim at a later date that witnesses would only pick him out of an identity parade because they had been prompted by seeing his picture in the newspaper.'

Reporter Gary Jones worked alongside Ian Edmundson to break the sensational news about Kenneth Noye. 'It was an exceptional story and everyone wanted a piece of it. Once we had that information confirmed, it was all guns blazing. Det Supt Biddiss was clearly shocked that we had this tip-off, and you could almost hear his brain whirring on the other end of the phone. You could sense him thinking, "This throws our investigation completely out of synch." His first reaction was that we couldn't possibly print the story because it would compromise identification. We knew from our sources that they were a long way off finding Kenny Noye and felt that by the time they did and had gone through extradition procedures it would be a long time after the photo was printed and that it would no longer be an issue. We certainly reigned back on quite a lot of the information we had, but felt it was in the public interest to run the story. Besides, they didn't have a clue where Kenny was, and one of our readers might have some valuable information.'

Biddiss realised that he would have to conduct the rest of the investigation on a need-to-know basis, as the leak about Kenneth Noye had to have come from within the police force. 'I knew there were people within the police organisation who were prepared to divulge confidential information to national newspapers, even about Kenneth Noye, a police killer.'

And the press were all too familiar with who these informants were. Gary Jones at *The News of the World* had spent years identifying and cultivating such contacts. 'It was bound to get out sooner rather than later. Some of the police are more leaky than a sieve. There are officers who can't wait to talk when they have good information on a case, even if it's just sharing that intelligence with their colleagues and friends. The more people that get to know about it, the further the news spreads, and eventually it reaches the press.'

Biddiss traced one of the leaks to the unethical distribution of an internal police publication. 'The Police Gazette is a confidential magazine to inform officers about particular crimes. It is intended purely for police sources. There was a small article carried in it informing officers that Kenneth Noye was wanted for questioning by the incident room. Someone in the police force passed a copy on to the press and the page was reproduced the next day in a national newspaper.'

Nick Biddiss was feeling the pressure. The press had revealed his hand and he had to regain control and prevent any further leaks about the investigation if he was to hold on to any chance of tracing Noye. But, unfortunately for the detective superintendent, when he tried to divert the media he suffered yet another embarrassing setback.

'We were holding a press conference and during the meeting I denied that we were seeking Kenneth Noye in relation to the murder of Stephen Cameron. Unfortunately, someone had left a plan of Noye's house on the wall behind me, and a reporter spotted it and asked me why it was there if Noye wasn't a suspect. With hindsight, we should have made sure it wasn't there.'

Ian Edmundson was shocked to hear that Det Supt Biddiss had called a press conference to deny the Kenneth Noye lead. 'He told the conference that The News of the World had got it wrong and then suddenly an eagle-eyed reporter asked why they had got an aerial photo of Kenneth Noye's house on the wall. Biddiss had little choice but to retreat and admitted that they did want to speak to Noye. It must have been really embarrassing for him. However, he chose his words very carefully and said that they wanted to interview Kenny Noye to eliminate him from their enquiries. He was never referred to as a chief suspect.'

The News of the World was already hot on the trail of Kenneth Noye. They followed up a tip-off that he was in hiding in Northern Cyprus, and Ian Edmundson was on the first plane to Istanbul to catch a connection to Cyprus. 'We were racing against time to try and find him in time for that weekend's edition, so that we could break the story that the police wanted to speak to Kenneth Noye and say that we had found him and put the allegations to him. While I was out on the ground, Gary was in the office compiling the background research and talking to the police.'

Noye was nowhere to be seen in Cyprus, although the news that he was there sent people who had been connected with him into panic. One customs officer who had previously arrested Noye, cancelled his summer vacation to the island because he feared for his safety if he were to bump into Noye. 'My wife and I were about to go on holiday to Cyprus, but it is a small place and I didn't know how Kenny Noye would react if he saw me. I could not take the risk.'

The failed Cyprus manhunt was the first of many trips for *The News of the World*, and in particular for Ian

Edmundson. Once the story was printed, calls came in thick and fast with information about where Kenneth Noye had been sighted. 'It got to the point where Kenneth Noye was being spotted on the moon. It was getting ludicrous. People were reporting that Noye was slipping in and out of the country, periodically returning to Britain to have a few beers with his friends and then hopping on a plane again.

Det Supt Biddiss was receiving similar information: 'There was a sighting at a Chinese restaurant in Kent, then another at a Caribbean restaurant in south London.' The bounty on Noye's head seemed to increase by the day, and newspapers were inundated with informants guaranteeing they could arrange a meeting with Noye for a price. Edmundson received a package from two private detectives containing plans and information that Noye was renting a windmill off an island near Tenerife. The package contained an aerial photograph of the windmill and details of a car Noye was alleged to be driving.

The press and police believed that Noye himself was responsible for some of the misleading tip-offs. Gary Jones received a call from a criminal source claiming that Noye was due to arrive back in the country on a small private plane. 'I duly went along and waited for him and, of course, he never turned up. The pilot, the plane and the company all existed. Everything was accurate apart from Kenneth Noye's part in it. It was a set-up. The criminal who tipped us off was probably put up to it by Noye to create confusion and diversion amongst the press and the police. I remember another time the police staked out the M25 expecting him to appear on the strength of a hoax tip-off.'

Det Supt Biddiss was informed of reported sightings on a daily basis in the initial stages of the murder inquiry, known as Operation Quern. After the first few months these petered out to around one a week and remained at that level until Noye's arrest two years after the incident. The locations varied from the sublime to the ridiculous. There were reported sightings of him in Kent, Milton Keynes, London, France, Morroco, Turkey and Norway. There were claims that he had bought a luxury villa in Lanzarote, was running a timeshare scam in Cyprus and was financing a drug-smuggling ring in Russia. There was even speculation that he planned to drastically alter his appearance with surgery and buy a ranch in Brazil.

'He couldn't possibly be in all these places but people genuinely believed they had seen him,' says Biddiss. 'Once we were told by a usually reliable police informant that Kenny Noye's best friend's daughter was getting married and that he wouldn't miss that wedding for the world. We attended but Noye didn't. We were told on another occasion that he was going to show his respects at an old friend's funeral. Information like this flooded in, and we went to more weddings and funerals than Hugh Grant, looking for Kenneth Noye, but he was never there.

'It was no joke at the time. The feeling amongst the public was that Kenneth Noye was repeatedly coming back into the country, right under the noses of the police and yet we couldn't catch him, even when he was socialising in our own back yard. In reality I don't think he ever came back into this country. He went abroad shortly after the incident and stayed there.'

Finally, after checking out leads in 13 different countries, there was a breakthrough. Biddiss was in his offices poring over the disparate intelligence the police had gathered, when the telephone rang. It was the incident room. They had received a tip-off about Kenneth Noye that sounded promising. Someone had reported seeing a British man fitting Noye's description living out on the Atlantic coast of Spain, in a community that was discreetly off the tourist track. Biddiss thought the information sounded worth following up. 'Criminals used to go to the Costa del Sol because of the opportunities there for them, hence its nickname, the Costa del Crime. Nowadays they know they are at risk of being spotted by a tourist, so they tend to go off the beaten track to avoid recognition. This person fitting Noye's description had drawn attention to himself because he didn't mix much, which was unusual for a British person trying to integrate into a new life abroad. By trying to be low-key he stood out.'

Former gangster and club owner Ronnie Knight knew only too well the risks of fleeing to Spain. 'Your mug shot is sent over there because the police think you've gone to Spain, or they know you've gone to Spain. So everyone out there is looking for you. You're in the papers over here and over there. Tourists go there on holiday and are bound to bump into you because you use the same places everyone else uses. It's only a matter of time before your number is up.'

The police have always maintained that the tip-off on Noye's hide-out in Spain came from a tourist, but underworld sources believe it was former gangland figure, Joey Wilkins, who betrayed Noye. Wilkins had fled to Spain after escaping from a British prison where he was serving a sentence for importing drugs. Criminal circles claim that Wilkins met up with Noye and later informed the British police that he was on the run in Cadiz. They say he became a police informant on the Costa Del Sol to safeguard his residence in Spain and avoid subsequent extradition to the UK. The police have always refuted this.

The police made some discreet undercover inquiries in the remote resort of Cadiz. Once they were satisfied that Noye was really there, they mobilised their officers. Det Supt Biddiss asked two of his officers to travel to Spain to try and locate Kenneth Noye. 'When you bear in mind that Noye had already killed a police officer and potentially one other person, it didn't sit easily with me, sending two of my men out there without back-up. All they had between them was a mobile phone and the assistance of a Spanish police officer based in Madrid. We were taking a huge gamble.

'I didn't fully comply with the protocols you are normally expected to go through with Interpol. There were only a handful of people who knew we were sending officers out there, and when it all came out later, an officer from Interpol did tear a strip off me, but by then we'd done what we needed to do.'

Two detectives volunteered for the job, but their discreet reconnaissance operation had to be kept secret from their families and colleagues. Even now, they have requested that their identities are not revealed. One of the officers who took part in the exercise recalls how initially he felt as if they were embarking on mission impossible. 'It just felt like we were looking for a needle in a haystack. We had an idea that Noye was staying in a village called Cadiz and we decided to concentrate our search from there, along the coastline, taking in several other villages along the way.

'For security and so as not to arouse suspicion, we were staying in a hotel 45 miles away, so we had an enormous amount of travelling to do each day. We wanted to keep ourselves as low-key as possible. In that region of Spain you get very few British tourists and we knew we would attract attention. We couldn't risk it because we didn't know what contacts [Noye] had made out there, and someone might have warned him that they had seen some people in the area who looked a bit suspicious. We didn't understand the language, it was incredibly hot and we spent a lot of time in the car driving around. It was a difficult and pressurised time for us. The only thing we had to work with was that Noye was driving a Blue Mitsubishi motor vehicle on red Belgium plates.'

The Spanish air was hot and dusty, and the officers – the two English men and their Spanish colleague – were thirsty and ready to take a break. They cruised steadily along the road, discussing how they could make best use of the rest of the day. About 30 yards ahead of them a blue vehicle pulled out from a side-track. All three men lurched forwards to get a better view. They turned to each other in amazement. It was Noye's vehicle. The Spanish driver followed the Mitsubishi and overtook it, enabling the other officers to take a close look at the driver. They confirmed it was Kenneth Noye.

'We couldn't believe it,' says one of the officers involved. 'Our time was almost up there, and then on our last day we had a positive sighting of him. We felt euphoric. After two years of searching, we had finally located Kenneth Noye. I don't think Det Supt Biddiss believed us at first. He had just received information of a sighting in Essex and he was more excited about that. I don't think he could take it in that we had finally found him after all that time.'

Det Supt Biddiss called a meeting with the officers as soon as they returned to England and, based on the information they provided, contacted the Crown Prosecution Service to discuss their next course of action. 'Stephen Cameron's fiancée, Danielle Cable, was the crux of the whole thing. She was the crucial eyewitness who could identify the man who stabbed her boyfriend. We needed to get her to identify him without him being aware of it before we could set the paperwork in motion to arrest him and bring him back to Britain.'

'Danielle was so vital to this enquiry. She was only 17 when she saw the man she was intending to spend the rest of her life with stabbed to death right before her eyes. She was brave and very determined to do whatever she had to to bring his murderer to justice.'

Biddiss recognised that the police would have to take Danielle to Spain to covertly identify Noye, but the exercise was fraught with danger. 'I needed to work out a plan where I could send Danielle with an identification officer to Spain and get them close enough to get a good look at Noye without compromising their safety or the integrity of the identification process. I had always told her that there was a possibility that she might have to go to a foreign country to identify the person responsible.'

However, to conceal the details from the press and to protect the safety of all those involved, the police didn't even tell Danielle that she was being taken to Spain. She met up with the identification officer believing that she was going to a location in the north of England, and several hours later found herself on a flight to Spain.

The identification officer (who cannot be named) was nervous about the trip. 'I thought, well, this is going to be a nightmare, taking out a member of the public who is a critical witness to a serious offence. You really have got to be careful of her welfare and your own. If our cover was blown and anything had gone wrong we would have been hung out to dry.

'Danielle was very young, with long blonde hair, and was extremely identifiable. I was much older than her, so she stood out when she was with me. We had a female Spanish chaperone with us and we would pretend that we were married and Danielle was our daughter. We were more convincing to look at as a family than as an older man accompanied on holiday by a much younger woman.

'Wherever we could, we had to keep [Danielle] in the car or wearing semi-disguise such as baseball caps and baggy tops. Sometimes we would even get her to change her clothes several times a day to alter her disguise, although this in itself can attract interest and reveal your true identity. So it all had to be carefully executed.'

For Danielle the visit to Spain was a strange mixture of excruciating boredom, sickening anticipation and blinding confusion. The identification officer was impressed by her approach to the bizarre situation she was thrust into. 'Although she was young, she had a very mature outlook, and despite the pressures and the stress she did everything we asked of her during the eight days we were out there. If we ordered her to duck down in the back seat because she was in danger of being exposed, she would do so without question. She didn't really have a clue what was going on because we couldn't brief her, and sometimes we would disappear for half a day and leave her with a chaperone and she never complained.

'The tension was high. We were continually looking over our shoulders. Even when we got back to the hotel in the evening we had to be careful about what we said because we didn't want to draw attention to ourselves. We hadn't arrived as part of a package holiday group, so we stood out. I felt added pressure because I had to worry about Danielle's safety as well as my own.'

The atmosphere was becoming strained. 'We knew our luck was running thin and that we couldn't keep following the suspect for much longer before someone recognised us and informed Noye or the press. The longer we stayed in Spain the more we increased our risks.

'We would venture out early in the morning and just drive aimlessly from one point to another. We would hang around for hours waiting for the suspect to appear, and sometimes there was no movement at all. He just wouldn't come out all day.

'I had to make sure that wherever we asked Danielle to view the suspect, it was in a reasonably crowded place. If it was too isolated, he could have claimed at a later date that she'd picked him out because there was nobody else around. I had to ensure that the identification procedure was fair for the suspect and safe for Danielle. If she had picked someone else out then we still would have brought her back the following day. We wouldn't have told her it was the wrong one because that would have been breaching the rules.

'There weren't many other English people around in the area where Kenneth Noye was living, so we had to spend a bit of time topping up our tans to ensure that we blended in with the crowd. The last thing we wanted to do was stand out like the milky white tourists who had just landed off the plane. The ideal scenario would have been to carry out the identification from the safety and anonymity of a car; however, most of the cars in southern Spain have tinted windows, and these are rarely wound down because the cars are air-conditioned, so that just wasn't an option.

'It was a logistical nightmare because so many things

could go wrong. We had to keep a constant eye out to make sure the press weren't on to us. I was well aware that they could take incriminating pictures from a distance undetectable to the human eye. We were looking for Noye but at the same time we were painfully aware that people could be watching us.'

After 30 years in the police force, this was the first time that this particular identification officer had had to travel to a foreign country to execute a covert identification. The exercise almost cost him his highly regarded reputation amongst friends, family and colleagues. Rumours were rife at the station when he failed to appear on duty. 'We weren't allowed to tell anyone where we were going, even our families. Half the force thought I'd been suspended and the other half thought I'd run off with another woman.

'My wife was getting anxious calls from my colleagues asking where I was, and she had to tell them that I'd left her. She even had to tell this story to her own mother, several other relatives and neighbours who were puzzled by my sudden disappearance. It was quite a burden for her because the rumours were awful.'

Det Supt Nick Biddiss couldn't do anything to help avert the gossip. 'Even my wife was getting on edge and wondering what was going on because I couldn't involve her. The officers who went out to Spain had a tough time because this kind of secrecy puts a strain on any relationship. I'm very pleased that these officers had understanding families because I was well aware of the tensions and strains I was subjecting them to.'

That the identification exercise remained a closely guarded secret was due to Nick Biddiss's meticulous planning. He knew that Kenneth Noye had a reputation for being able to influence and corrupt some police officers. Noye openly fraternised with them and relied on his connections as a Freemason to bail him out of trouble. Years earlier, Detective Sergeant John Donald had tipped off Noye and an associate that they were under surveillance by a US Drugs Enforcement Agency. (The officer had also accepted bribes from other criminals and was later jailed for 11 years, convicted of corruption.) Det Supt Biddiss knew there might well be other officers like Donald who would warn Noye that he was being watched. He wasn't prepared to take any chances and kept his investigative procedures tightly under wraps right up to Noye's arrest.

Eight days into the exercise, the team in Spain experienced a stroke of luck. The officers spotted Noye's car leaving his villa in Silver Bay and tailed it to the Il Forna restaurant in La Muela, 15 miles away. Noye was speeding adeptly along the familiar Spanish roads, making it hard for the convoy to keep up behind. The identification officer knew that this was probably going to be their best shot at nailing Kenneth Noye. 'We started to tail the vehicle, which was driving at about 80 miles per hour, and I warned Danielle that I was taking her to a place where we would see a group of people and she might recognise the man who stabbed Stephen.

Danielle sat apprehensively and cast her mind back to that dreadful day, hardly believing that within minutes she could be face to face with Stephen's murderer again. The Spanish officer was talking on the telephone in Spanish to the two officers in the car in front. Realising that they were conversing in Spanish to prevent her from understanding what was about to happen, Danielle turned anxiously to the identification officer, saying, 'I don't know what the bloody hell is going on.' He looked at her sympathetically. For him this could be the turning point of the trip, but for her it was a road riddled with angst and soul-destroying memories. 'Well, you remember that feeling of not knowing what is going on,' he reassured her. 'One day people will accuse you of knowing exactly what was going on and being party to a set-up of the suspect.' It was little comfort for Danielle.

Their car pulled up outside the hillside pasta restaurant. The identification officer spotted the suspect's car parked nearby. Noye was definitely there. They changed hastily into the formal clothes they had stored in the car, and the identification officer pulled Danielle to one side: 'I told her that we weren't going to be able to leave her in the car. That she was going to have to go into the restaurant and look at every person in there and that she was at risk of being recognised. I think she had about 30 seconds to think about it and then we were walking in.'

The restaurant was crowded and there were no seats available. Danielle and the two officers accompanying her felt incongruous. She glanced about nervously, barely able to distinguish any of the sea of faces bobbing around her. The meaningless sound of chatter and laughter droned in her ears as she cut her way through the mass of diners. The officer spotted a small window and guided Danielle towards it. Gently he told her to stand beside it and look through it as if searching for a spare seat. She felt slightly faint and light-headed in the heat; her legs beginning to wobble now that she was faced with the reality of possibly being in the same room as the murderer. She lifted her head and glanced through the window. On her second glance to her right she noticed a bench table with a party of diners laughing and joking. She felt a thud in the pit of her stomach. Her brain registered the features of a man with a distinctive broken nose sitting at the end of the table, laughing loudly with his companions. Her memory sped back two years and registered the same face, wild and contorted, as the man ferociously stabbed her fiancé to death and then sauntered away smiling. An icy chill surged through her body. She swayed slightly, feeling that her legs were about to collapse beneath her.

She turned to the identification officer: 'Yes, he's there. His hair is lighter but it is him.' The officer confirmed the person she was referring to and then checked with the Spanish officer to ensure that he was happy with the identification.

'Danielle was visibly distressed and I needed to get her out of the restaurant before she broke down. I told her we would have to casually walk past his party as we left the restaurant. I kept hoping that no one from his table would look up and notice the tears in her eyes. It seemed to take forever to get out of that place. We couldn't even look back in case someone from Noye's table glanced up and pointed us out. Once we were through the door and into the car park, we more or less lifted Danielle off the ground and got her into the car.

'I couldn't tell Danielle whether she had identified our suspect or not, as this would have breached the rules, so although I was ecstatic I couldn't show any reaction. We got her back to the hotel so that she could have a good cry and spend some time coming to terms with what she had just experienced. It must have been very traumatic for her. It was a difficult encounter, but she was brave throughout.

'Once we were back at the hotel, I drafted out a handwritten report of what had happened, and then in the early hours of the morning we persuaded the receptionist to fax it to Det Supt Biddiss, making her promise not to read it. Back in Britain Biddiss waited for the crucial document to arrive. The Spanish team had phoned through to say that it had been sent, but there was no sign of it in Biddiss's office.

The team in Spain finally relaxed, safe in the knowledge that their job was done and everything had gone to plan. They were preparing to take a flight back to the UK when they received an unexpected telephone call. 'Det Supt Biddiss rang us and said that the fax hadn't arrived, and we were all thrown into a wild panic wondering where on earth this highly confidential report had got to. We started to imagine that it had found its way into the wrong hands and were getting quite concerned, then, fortunately, [Biddiss] realised that he had forgotten to switch the machine on and phoned us back to apologise.' Biddiss flicked the power switch and stood impatiently, waiting for the document to expel from the roller.

He says, 'Receiving that fax was the eureka moment we had all been waiting for. Finally, we had found the man responsible for Stephen Cameron's murder and we had managed to identify him without any harm to the chief witness. At first I had a few moments of doubt, wondering if they really had seen him. We had worked so hard and long for this moment that when it arrived I could scarcely believe it. There were times while they were out there when I had seriously considered bringing them home, and I'm so glad I didn't. Now I had evidence that he was the culprit, I could apply for a warrant from a magistrate and have him arrested in Spain.'

Noye was enjoying an al fresco meal with a striking female companion, Min Al Taiba, at the bustling El Campero restaurant in Barbate. It was a beautiful mid-August evening in the quaint tuna-fishing village. Noye had just eaten a salad starter followed by red mullet, and 38-year-old Min had ordered a local fish dish, the dorada. They were contemplating the dessert menu when four undercover detectives dressed in shorts and t-shirts ran over, pinned Noye to the ground and snapped on handcuffs. Britain's most wanted man had been arrested.

Det Supt Nick Biddiss was approaching his retirement, and catching Noye was the best departing gift he could receive to mark his days in the police force. He flew out to Spain and spent his last three weeks in the job sorting out Kenneth Noye's extradition papers and thanking the Spanish officers who had assisted with the operation.

Gary Jones at *The News of the World* was amazed by the news of Noye's arrest. 'The press would have loved to have been there when he was caught. The fact that the police were able to track him down and arrest him in a foreign country without him or anyone else knowing anything about it was quite a coup. It was a spectacular operation and you have to hand it to Biddiss, he really did get one over on the press. We didn't have a clue about it until it was all over.

'As for Noye, well he had acquired a sort of Lord Lucan status while he was in hiding. He was a complex and sophisticated criminal on the run from justice and for a long time he managed to outrun the police and the press. Even though he is serving a life sentence I suspect that there are people on the outside who are still working for Kenneth Noye in some form or other.'

The day after the arrest, Noye appeared before magistrates in Cadiz, but he wasn't willing to return to Britain to face charges without a fight. He immediately launched an appeal against his extradition. His lawyer, Henry Milner, told an extradition hearing in Madrid that Noye's arrest was illegal and that he would not have a fair trial in the UK because he had already undergone trial by the media. His appeal against the extradition was rejected by a panel of judges and Noye made his first British court appearance two months later at Dartford Magistrates' Court with armed police surrounding the building. He was remanded to Belmarsh prison in south-east London, pending trial by jury.

Jon Saunders returned from a camping trip in Holland to hear that Kent Police had been looking for him. 'I thought, Oh my God, what have I done? What is this about.' The police contacted him again and made an appointment to visit him at home. 'An officer came round and told me that Kenneth Noye had been arrested and that they were going to charge him with the murder of Stephen Cameron. He explained that I would be required to give evidence in court and warned me that if I received any strange telephone calls or suspicious callers at the house, then I was to contact the police straightaway. He even mentioned a witness protection scheme if things became difficult. I thought it was a bit over the top and didn't pay too much attention to it.'

A few months later Jon Saunders was invited to attend an identity parade in west London to formally identify Kenneth Noye. Jon arrived at Kilburn station and was shocked to see the building surrounded by armed officers. 'They were on the roof, in the courtyard, by the exits, just about everywhere. The place was swarming with them. At that point I wondered if there really was something for me to worry about.'

Jon and the other witnesses were led into the identity suite, where they were asked to look at 12 people through mirrored glass and see if they could identify the person at the scene of the crime. 'I was asked to walk up and down twice to make sure I had a good view, but as soon as I saw Noye I knew that he was the one.'

After Noye's arrest, detectives discovered that while on the run he had continued with his criminal activities. They uncovered evidence that suggested Noye had used a false passport to travel to Tangiers and Jamaica for drug deals, and then to Aruba in the Dutch Antilles, where he was suspected of setting up false accounts. They also traced dealings with the Mafia in the US. Noye has never been formally charged with any of these alleged offences.

From the time of his arrest to his trial, Kenneth Noye declined to speak to the police. He finally stood trial at the Old Bailey in April 2000, charged with the murder of Stephen Cameron. In a bitter twist, his trial was heard in the same courtroom where, 15 years earlier, he had been cleared of murdering undercover detective John Fordham.

While in Spain Noye had firmly denied being involved in the M25 murder, but once back in Britain he conceded that he had stabbed Stephen Cameron but claimed once again he had acted in self-defence.

Det Supt Biddiss was shocked by his plea: 'I was surprised that Kenneth Noye mentioned self-defence, especially as he must have known that certain key witnesses had failed to identify him from photographs, so I thought that rather than plead self-defence he was more likely to challenge the identification in Spain.'

John Mathews QC, who had represented Kenneth Noye during his trial for the murder of police officer John Fordham, was also surprised by Noye's self-defence plea. 'I couldn't believe that Noye had been so incredibly stupid as to get involved in a road rage episode that resulted in someone's death and then say it was self-defence. He had a major problem because here was somebody who had killed twice with a knife and both times he pleaded he was acting in self-defence. He was up against it because, although coincidences do happen, it was a lot for a jury to accept.'

The barrister was also concerned that Noye's notoriety had finally caught up with him. 'There had been endless publicity for a year, labelling him as a dangerous man and referring back to his acquittal over the killing of the police officer, so I think there is a grave question mark over whether Kenneth Noye could ever really have had a fair trial.'

Jon Saunders was shocked by Noye's appearance when he came face to face with him in court. 'I couldn't believe it was the same person. He looked like a little, frail, old man. His hair was grey and he was wearing a grey cardigan. He looked wizened and dishevelled, and you wouldn't believe he would say boo to a goose. I thought that it was all an act and that he was trying to fool the jury into thinking he was a frail, elderly man. I saw him stab Stephen Cameron and he wasn't a frail man then.' Noye wore the same grey cardigan throughout the 12-day trial.

Jon Saunders hoped the jury wouldn't be taken in by Noye's calculated appearance. 'I prayed that the jury would see through his act. It was very important to me that he was found guilty because I saw him commit the crime. It is a day I will never forget and I hope I never have to see another person die for such a pointless reason. He took a man's life and you cannot repay that by letting him walk free.'

The court heard how, minutes after the killing, Noye rang his wife Brenda and a number of other associates. He called on his extensive network of criminal contacts to help him dispose of the Land Rover, collect a suitcase stuffed with £10,000 of cash and flee the country. He telephoned fraudster John 'Goldfinger' Palmer (later jailed for eight years for cheating thousands of holiday-makers in a timeshare fraud in the Canary Islands), who arranged for him to be flown by helicopter to a golf course near Caen, Normandy. From there he travelled by train to Paris and caught Palmer's private jet to Madrid. Then he moved on to the Canary Islands, where he stayed for a few days at Palmer's villa in Lanzarote. He later travelled into southern Spain, where he bought a sumptuous villa in Silver Bay, Cadiz.

To ensure that he could move freely between countries he used a passport in the name of Alan Edward Green, which some interpreted as a joke at the expense of Allan Green, the Director of Public Prosecutions at the time.

Julian Bevan QC, acting for the prosecution, said that Cameron's murder was born out of 'anger and pride' resulting from a punch-up between the two men, and that within minutes of the attack Noye set about covering his tracks and fleeing the country with his suitcase full of cash.

Danielle Cable told the court: 'I saw his knife and I was pleading with him not to hurt Steve and I couldn't go near him because I felt he would harm me. I saw

Steve clutch his chest. He said, "He stabbed me, Dan. Take his number plate." I saw blood on his chest. It was dreadful. I was screaming and crying for someone to help me. Then Stephen collapsed on the floor.'

Pathologist Dr Michael Heath used a plastic ruler to demonstrate on a court usher how Noye twice rammed the blade up to the hilt with great force, puncturing Stephen's heart and liver.

Another witness told the court how he saw the glint of the blade before Noye thrust it hard into Stephen Cameron's chest. Jon Saunders told them how Noye had driven off after the attack with a look 'as if to say that's sorted him out'.

Noye said that he stabbed Cameron after the 21-year-old electrician had flown at him in a 'wild rage' during a simple misunderstanding. Eyewitnesses gave conflicting evidence about who started the fight. Heather Titley said she saw Cameron grab Noye's shirt collar and scuffle with him. Helen Merral also said Cameron landed the first blow. But Stephen Darling testified that Noye had struck Cameron first, hitting him in the face with his right fist. 'That was definitely the first action of violence when they met,' said Mr Darling. But, he went on to say – in a version of events that corroborated Noye's account – 'The younger fellow was getting the better of the older one. I saw him throw punches and he was kicking. The older bloke was backing off. I thought the older fellow got out to give the younger one a clout, then the young one got the better of him. I thought, fair enough, he deserves it.'

The jury of eight women and four men took more than

eight hours to reach its 11 to one verdict of guilty. Lord Justice Latham said: 'The jurors have found you guilty of murder and, as you know, there is only one sentence I can impose, and that is life imprisonment. I don't propose to say anything more at this stage.'

As the verdict was announced, Stephen Cameron's parents, Toni and Ken, leapt up at the back of the court clasping each other's hands and shouting, 'Yes!' After the hearing they released a statement to the waiting media: 'We are happy that justice for Stephen has been done, but this is not a joyous occasion. Our lovely son Stephen is dead and our lives will never be the same again. We are still experiencing overwhelming grief, as any parents who have lost a child will understand.'

Ken Cameron, a manager for a cleaning company, later described to journalists the torment he and his family had endured during the four years since the murder. He revealed that he had been unable to sleep for several days and had not worked since his son was killed in 1996. 'It cost me my job. I just couldn't cope with the pressure of it. It's the price you have to pay. Perhaps now we can get on with the rest of our lives, hopefully.'

The now retired Det Supt Nick Biddiss was also thrilled by the verdict. 'I'd lived through this nightmare with Danielle and Stephen's parents, Ken and Toni. When Noye was convicted they were jumping up and down in court, bursting with relief that justice had finally been served. It helped them to move on, and I was thrilled that the criminal justice system worked, despite Noye trying to exploit its loopholes.'

Detective Supt Dennis McGookin, who took over the Cameron case after Nick Biddiss retired, told the media that Stephen's family and friends had been to hell and back. He added: 'Today's verdict clearly shows that you can run from justice but you cannot hide. Noye thought he was above the law and would never go to court.'

Danielle Cable wasn't in court for the verdict but was telephoned by police, who informed her of the conviction. 'When the officer phoned me from court to tell me about the guilty verdict I was overjoyed. I could not believe it at first. But it will never bring back my Steve. I just hope he's looking down from heaven today and smiling. This is for him.' Danielle was forced to assume a new identity because of fears that Noye's underworld associates might seek vengeance and harm her. She radically altered her appearance, changed her name and moved to another part of the country. Before and during the trial she was only allowed to contact her family via a mobile telephone.

The Chief Crown Prosecutor for Kent, Elizabeth Howe, was full of praise for the team who helped to bring Noye to justice: 'This was a savage killing and were it not for the prosecution teamwork, Kenneth Noye would still be enjoying a comfortable lifestyle on the Costa del Sol.'

Case officer DI Terry Garbriel revealed after the trial that Noye's own stubbornness prevented him from avoiding conviction: 'The biggest mistake Noye made in the latter days was to fight his extradition from Spain. Had he returned voluntarily we could have been in serious trouble because of the restrictions surrounding how long you can detain someone. It may have meant that much of the groundwork we did that forced Noye into a corner might not have been completed on time. The trial might then have taken a very different course.'

One of the trial witnesses whom Jon Saunders met during the identity parade was Alan Decabral. He had witnessed the murder and followed Noye's vehicle for a while to try to note down his registration number and see which direction he was travelling in. He was a key witness for the prosecution, telling the court: 'I saw the knife go into [Stephen's] chest. I saw the blood. I'll never forget his face.' These words condemned Alan Decabral to a life of fear. He had shunned police witness protection in the months before and after the trial, and within half a year of giving evidence he was shot dead.

Decabral was sitting in his black Peugeot 206 on the Warren Retail Park in Kent when a man in his twenties walked over, pulled out a gun and fired a single fatal shot into Decabral's head. His 18-year-old son, Adam, discovered his limp, blood-spattered body on his return to the car.

Jon Saunders was stunned by the news of the shooting: 'I remember hearing on the radio that there had been a fatal shooting outside a shop in Ashford. The victim was Alan Decabral and the media were linking the shooting to him being a key witness in the Kenneth Noye trial.' Noye's reputation as a character not to be messed with was still riding high in the media, even though he was securely behind bars. *The Sun* newspaper also alleged that Noye had issued a £60,000 contract on Danielle Cable's life.

Decabral had claimed after the trial: 'I look over my shoulder every time I go into the supermarket.' Witnesses to his shooting in Ashford claimed they heard him beg: 'Please don't kill me, please don't shoot,' seconds before the gunman fired. Decabral had also claimed after the trial that he had received repeated threats intended to prevent him from giving evidence, claiming on one occasion that three bullets had been posted through his letter-box. The police have no record of him reporting the incident.

Saunders was shaken by news of the shooting: 'When I got home I received calls from police checking that I was okay. A detective visited me and said they were putting on extra foot patrols on the estate where I lived. He gave me an emergency telephone number that guaranteed me an instant response if I ran into any trouble. They even told my partner she could have a panic button installed to protect her while I was out at work. At the back of my mind I convinced myself that the shooting was just a co-incidence, but the police weren't going to take any chances.'

Bob McCunn, a lawyer who had been working to recover losses from the gold bullion trial, was familiar with the dangers to be considered when dealing with Kenneth Noye and his associates: 'When we started the investigation we took advice on security measures we should take. We would sweep the office occasionally for bugs. If we felt that someone was following us then we would report it to the police. There were occasions of intimidation. We were dealing with villains of varying degrees of unpleasantness. One investigator had a quantity of drugs planted in his hotel room while he was in Spain. Fortunately, he was tipped off and headed for the nearest airport before the drugs were discovered.

'Somebody else was out one day and a man pulled his jacket aside to reveal a gun and holster. It was a warning. Another individual was investigating in the United States and we were informed that a contract had been taken out on him. It was sufficient intelligence for us to make further inquires through the FBI to check it out.' None of this could be directly linked to Noye, but it involved people involved in the theft and disposal of gold bullion, which Noye had been convicted for being a party to.

The police never established any concrete evidence to link Noye with Alan Decabral's murder, but as a precaution they offered round-the-clock protection for the other 12 witnesses in the Kenneth Noye trial. The truth was that Decabral was also a villain. He had a criminal history that included drug smuggling and trading in firearms, and the police believed that he could have made a number of enemies who had a motive to kill him.

It is hardly surprising, given his criminal background, that Decabral had rejected police protection. Having a police officer looking over his shoulder would have been bad for business. All the same, he was armed with emergency numbers to call if he ran into trouble, but they provided little protection against a contract killer.

The suspicion that Noye had ordered the shooting did little for his public profile, but undeterred he continued with an appeal against his conviction for murdering

Stephen Cameron. He launched the appeal on the grounds that Alan Decabral, a key prosecution witness, had a criminal background, and Noye claimed that he had lied in the witness box.

Noye's lawyer, Michael Mansfield QC, claimed that Decabral was a criminal who 'embellished his account to take in things he had never seen' in an attempt to win favour with the police. He suggested that Decabral's reward came in 1999, when he escaped prosecution on a drugs charge.

He also alleged that excessive publicity concerning Noye's involvement with crime had prejudiced any chance of a fair trial. Lord Chief Justice Woolf, sitting with Justices Douglas Brown and Astill, dismissed the appeal on all grounds. Lord Woolf said there was 'no justification for Noye taking out a knife, opening it and using it in the fracas with Mr Cameron'.

Noye was reminded that there were 22 other witnesses that day, including 18 with a reliable view of the incident, and that their testimonies were as valid as Alan Decabral's. Regarding the publicity, Lord Woolf said that juries could usually put out of their minds media comment that could be prejudicial. The court ruled that Noye had had a fair trial and that the conviction was sound. Noye showed no emotion as he was led back to the cells, but the appeal brought painful memories to the surface for Stephen's parents once again.

Outside the court, Ken Cameron vented his emotions. 'Kenneth Noye tried to destroy Stephen's name again and I think that's outrageous. I hope he spends the rest of his life in jail. I hope he comes out in a wooden box.' Mrs Cameron was also deeply distressed by Noye's appeal. 'I feel hatred. He has destroyed our lives. I hope life means life. He had a knife and used it and he should pay for it.'

Det Supt Nick Biddiss sympathises with Stephen's parents. 'I think Noye's reputation has overshadowed the memory of Stephen Cameron to a certain extent. I'd like people to remember Stephen, rather than the name Kenneth Noye.'

Since the trial, Danielle Cable has maintained her new identity under the witness protection programme.

4 GIRLSNATCHER

It was a beautiful August day in 2001 and a young man was strolling through Lindley Woods, an unexpected oasis of peace just outside industrial, urban Leeds. Mark was familiar with the woods and walked there regularly, but this time, as he passed some trees, he noticed an uneven mound of disturbed earth which he was sure hadn't been there before. Everything else appeared familiar, but this was definitely new.

He hesitantly investigated and discovered what looked like a bundle of bedclothes half buried in a shallow grave. Fearing the worst, Mark prodded the fabric with a branch and then prised the floral duvet cover apart. Inside was a package tightly wrapped in bin liners. Disturbed and frightened, Mark decided that it was probably a dead pet and backed slowly away to continue his walk.

However, he couldn't get the thought of what he had found in the woods out of his mind. He even joked with his partner, Ann, that he had stumbled across a human corpse. But the jest haunted him and the following day he felt compelled to return to the scene and face his fear. Once again, he tentatively toyed with the mysterious bundle, but he soon realised that he would have to forcibly rip it open if he was to find out what was inside. Once again, he convinced himself that it had to be a dog, and he uneasily made his way home.

That evening, he could think of little else but the package. He sought reassurance from friends to try to quell his anxiety. He was sure the package was too small to be a human, and as he attempted to emulate the size, he folded his arms across his chest, tucked in his chin and drew his knees up. Suddenly, he realised that a large body could actually appear quite small, and it was at this point that Mark decided he had to go to the police, if only to put his mind at rest.

The following day Mark cautiously directed a bemused police officer to the obscure bundle stashed in Lindley Woods. Pulling out a small pocket-knife, the officer carefully sliced apart the plastic liners, expectantly peeling back the layers. This seemed to take a lifetime, but suddenly Mark reeled backwards as he saw the top of a sock showing through the confines of the plastic bandaging.

Steadying himself he glanced wide-eyed at the officer as they both absorbed the grim knowledge that Mark had indeed discovered human remains. 'It was tremendously shocking because I never expected to find something so disturbing in such a beautiful environment. A place I had visited several times a week for a long time,' Mark later told the police.

The officer radioed for back up and within 20 minutes the usually tranquil woodland retreat was swarming with police and forensic experts, covered head to foot like bee-keepers in bulging white coveralls. Mark felt numb and struggled to come to terms with his grisly discovery. 'Even then I still couldn't believe I had found a body. It just didn't seem possible.' For the police it was a major breakthrough, marking the conclusion of an arduous nine-month search for missing schoolgirl Leanne Tiernan – and the beginning of a testing murder inquiry.

Leanne was a vibrant 16-year-old who lived with her divorced mother on the sprawling Landseer estate in the Bramley area of Leeds. She had overcome a heart defect as a small child to blossom into a confident, healthy and popular teenager. She was especially close to her mother, Sharon Hawkhead and her sister, Michelle, who was three years older. They jokingly called themselves 'the three Musketeers' and, even though Michelle had moved out of the family home two years earlier, the inseparable trio still spent most weekends together, watching videos, drinking wine and playing music.

Leanne was studying for nine GCSEs at West Leeds High School and was affectionately known by her uncle as his Chocolate Chip Niece, because of her insatiable love of chocolate. Like other teenage girls, Leanne enjoyed chatting about fashion and boys, listening to dance music and going shopping with her friend Sarah Whitehouse. 'We'd known each other for six years and used to spend a lot of time at each other's houses or as a foursome with our boyfriends. We were typical teenagers in every sense. Leanne was so bubbly and funny. She really used to make me laugh. The day she went missing I'd called her to see if she wanted to go Christmas shopping in town for a couple of hours.'

There was little to amuse teenagers in Landseer on a Sunday afternoon and Leanne didn't need any persuading. 'Mum, please can I borrow some money to buy Sarah's Christmas present? We're going into town and I'm broke. I'll pay you back in a few weeks,' she pleaded. Sharon smiled and reached for her purse, pulling out £11 she'd been saving to pay some bills. 'Here, that should be enough. Have a nice time and be back for 5 pm in time for dinner.'

'Thanks mum. I'll be home on time,' Leanne promised as she breezed out of the door, kissing Sharon lightly and giggling at the lipstick stain she had left imprinted on her mother's cheek.

The girls darted in and out of the Leeds city centre shops, attempting to dodge the icy November rain while they searched for a navel bar and a wishbone ring for Sarah's Christmas present before boarding the bus for the three-mile journey home.

They stepped off the bus together to make arrangements to meet up again later that evening. As they reached Sarah's road, they parted company and Sarah watched Leanne walk off into the distance. It was the last time she would see her friend alive.

The air was damp and biting and Leanne was no doubt eager to escape the cold and reach the warmth of her home. It would be quicker to take a short cut through the secluded wooded valley of Houghley Gill rather than walking along the well-lit main road. Although she had repeatedly been warned by her family to avoid the dense woodland walk, Leanne was familiar with the route and as she was in a hurry to get home would have calculated she could cut ten minutes off her journey. It was an ill-fated decision.

Sharon Hawkhead was feeling anxious. It was already 5.20 pm and Leanne was rarely late. She glanced from the clock to the window and back to the clock again. Surely any minute Leanne would burst through the door full of apologies for being delayed? The telephone rang. Startled Sharon swung around and lifted the receiver expecting to hear Leanne's voice. 'Hi, it's Sarah. Can I speak to Leanne please?' requested the caller. Sharon was taken aback. If Leanne wasn't with Sarah, where was she?

Sarah was also astounded to hear that Leanne wasn't at home. 'When I arrived home my boyfriend rang to see if we wanted to go to his house so I thought I'd give Leanne 15 minutes to arrive home and then I'd call her. I was really shocked when her mum said that she wasn't there.'

Concerned, Sharon asked Sarah exactly where and when they had parted company. Beginning to panic, she decided to call Leanne on her mobile telephone. The familiar ring tone droned 20 times then cut off abruptly. On her second attempt the telephone diverted straight to Leanne's answering service. Thinking that for some unknown reason Leanne was avoiding her, Sharon asked Sarah to try, but Sarah was also immediately connected to

Leanne's recorded message: 'Hi, it's Leanne. I can't get to the phone right now. Call back later. Bye.' Sarah bit her lip. Something was terribly wrong.

Sharon cast her mind back to earlier that day. There was no indication that Leanne had left the house on bad terms or was planning to run away. 'As she walked out the door she gave me the usual kiss on the cheek which left a lipstick mark on my face. She laughed about it and left the house full of beans. She'd been to church with her grandparents that morning and on her return she decided to go into town with Sarah to do some shopping. I couldn't see any reason why she might have run away. We hadn't had any rows. There were no bad feelings between us. It just didn't make sense.'

Michelle and her boyfriend Darren, who were joining Sharon and Leanne for their Sunday evening meal, offered to search the neighbourhood with the two family dogs. Sharon wracked her brain for a rational explanation for Leanne's strange disappearance. 'Leanne was wearing some new boots that day and she wasn't very good in heels. I thought maybe she had fallen somewhere and broken her leg or sprained her ankle and couldn't get to the phone.'

It was still early evening but darkness had already fallen and it was pitch black. The soft halo of the street lighting did little to illuminate any hiding places and the rain shot through the dark in fierce torrents, forming streams that flowed rapidly towards the gaping drains. Michelle and Darren trawled the shadowy streets, stopping scurrying passers-by as they hurried to escape the rainfall. 'Sorry to bother you, but have you seen a 16-year-old girl with dark, shoulder length hair and an eyebrow ring?' they queried hopefully. No one had seen her.

Michelle felt a strong sense of foreboding. 'At first we searched the way she would have walked home. We were hoping that we would find her talking to someone and that she had lost track of time. After about an hour we started to panic because there was just no sign of her.' The rain continued to come down hard, drenching their clothes and soaking them to the bone. Caked in mud, they wearily ventured home to collect a torch for their search of Houghley Gill. It was a last resort. 'The rain was pelting down and we had to return home to change our clothes five times. We searched for most of the night, particularly around Houghley Gill because that was the darkest and loneliest place she could have walked along.'

'Leanne, are you there?' they called, slowly arcing the torch in front of them. There was no reply, other than the crackle of bushes being blown in the wind. The lights of nearby houses penetrated through the trees like staring eyes, watching, waiting. 'Let's get out of here!' Michelle whispered. 'She's not here and there are other places we can search.'

While the couple extended their trawl along the nearby canal bank, Leanne's mother called on friends and neighbours and Leanne's boyfriend, Wayne Keeley, to join the expanding search party. Sharon began to face the possibility that Leanne had walked through the Gill rather than along the main road. 'Houghley Gill is quite wooded and I didn't like Leanne using it, but it is surrounded by housing and lots of people do use it everyday. You see people doing drugs deals down there or occasionally dumping a stolen car, but as long as you walk straight past them they don't bother you. Being a fearless teenager, Leanne clearly wasn't concerned about walking through it, even after dark.'

Her father, Michael Tiernan, had also advised her not to use the Gill. 'My mother never used to like me walking through it and as I got older I realised the dangers. I always told Leanne that it was safer to take the long way around on the main road when she was travelling to and from her friend's house. But when you're young you don't have any concept of danger and just see it as an easy short cut.'

'Don't you think it's time you called the Police?' Sharon's fiancé, William, suggested gently after hours of fruitless searching. Sharon nodded and reached for the telephone. 'I knew in my heart that if she didn't walk through the door by 10 pm then she wouldn't be coming home at all.'

Family, friends and police continued to search for Leanne throughout the night, and Michelle and Darren came unwittingly close to the scene of her death. They abandoned their foot search and took the car so they could hunt further afield. Slowly, they circled the housing estate, directing their headlights into the darkness like a searchlight. Darren spotted another opening and steered the vehicle down an alleyway not far from Sarah Whitehouse's home. There were several allotments backing on to a line of terraced houses and they wondered if Leanne was sheltering from the rain in one of the ramshackle outbuildings.

They combed the area meticulously, calling out her name, but there was no one to be seen or heard. Climbing back into the car, Darren pressed the accelerator but the wheels just span frantically beneath them while the vehicle remained stubbornly motionless. Eerily they were trapped in the mud, just yards from the house where Leanne was being held. Michelle was devastated when she later learned how close she had been to finding her captive sister.

'It was pretty sickening to find out later on that we had been so close and never realised it. In hindsight it was as if someone had been trying to tell us that she was only feet away. It was like some kind of a supernatural message, but unfortunately we didn't recognise it at the time.'

Leanne's father, Michael Tiernan, was holidaying in Tenerife when he heard that his daughter had been reported missing. 'At first I didn't think too much of it. I thought that she had had an argument with someone and was sulking somewhere.'

But the police suggested that Michael Tiernan should return to Leeds immediately and he spent the following night at the airport trying to board an earlier flight home. 'It wasn't until I returned to England that I realised how serious the situation was. There were police cars all over the estate looking for her and rubbish was piled up in the street because the police had delayed the refuse collection so they could search it for clues.' Feeling helpless, Michael joined the intense search and, armed with a photograph of Leanne, he went knocking on doors asking if anyone had seen his missing daughter.

'Everyone who had anything to do with Leanne was a suspect. The day after I returned from holiday the police told me they would have to search my house. Fifteen policemen turned the place upside down, from the loft to the garage. That's when it really came home to me that they thought she had probably been killed and we were all in the frame.'

Det Supt Chris Gregg joined the investigation on day three. 'Girls of Leanne's age do go missing, but you usually find something in their background fairly quickly that explains why they have run away. Leanne was from a stable family and appeared to be a bright and happy teenager, so we couldn't see any reason why she would disappear of her own accord. There were no signs of a secret boyfriend or clues that she had got involved with a bad crowd. We were also disturbed by the fact that her mobile phone had been switched off when her mother tried to call her. That suggested to us that darker forces were involved.'

With no obvious explanation for Leanne's disappearance the police asked Sharon Hawkhead to appeal for information at a press conference. But Sharon felt too emotionally fragile to handle the media interest and Michelle bravely offered to take her place. 'My mum was just too distraught so I agreed to do it. It was the scariest thing I have ever had to do. I didn't know what to expect and I was still in shock over Leanne's disappearance. I'm sure Leanne would have got in touch if she had been watching. If she had run away she wouldn't have put her family through that pain and would have contacted us to let us know that she was okay.'

Michelle, Sharon and Leanne's grandmother, Hilary Hawkhead, endured another agonising press conference just days later and on his return to the country Michael Tiernan, Leanne's father, also volunteered to make a press appeal. 'It was overwhelming. You walk in and see all these cameras and microphones set up and people are clambering over each other shouting questions and taking pictures. You just freeze. It's an unpleasant but necessary process to endure. We had to take every opportunity of making contact with Leanne or anyone who might be holding her.'

On the same day as the press conference, Gregg also organised a reconstruction of Leanne's final movements before she disappeared. Due to her physical resemblance, Michelle agreed to pose as Leanne making her last journey home. 'I hadn't used Houghley Gill since that night so it was painful for me to walk through there, but I felt it was worth it if it reminded someone who might have seen her.

'Although she was my younger sister she was a lot taller than me. Apart from that we looked very much alike. I dressed in similar clothes, trimmed my fringe, dyed my hair brown and pinned it up like Leanne's. The worst thing was putting my eyebrow ring back in. We both had one but I had taken mine out. I walked through the kitchen door at my mum's and she nearly fainted because for a few seconds she thought it was Leanne coming home.'

'Leanne and I were like chalk and cheese and in many respects we became a lot closer after I moved out. She was such an outgoing girl who was very bubbly and confident. She loved rock and dance music and was a typical fun-loving teenager. She was one of those kids who would always play her music really loud and constantly be laughing and joking. Now the house seems so quiet without her.

'I convinced myself that she must have run away because the alternative was too unbearable to contemplate. But in reality, Leanne was one of those people who couldn't keep something like that to herself and I think I knew deep down that something awful had happened to her but I didn't want to face it.'

Leanne's friend, Sarah Whitehouse was persuaded by the police to join Michelle in the reconstruction. 'People were taking photographs and I just felt numb and detached. It was agonising replaying what we had done that day but I wanted her to come home so badly that I agreed to take part.

'I found it difficult to comprehend that the police were out looking for my friend. It was all such a blur. Sometimes when the police asked me questions I felt like I was being interrogated. It was as if they thought that I knew where she was and wasn't prepared to say so. They came to my house and questioned me nearly every day for a fortnight. I was only 15 and had no experience of the police so I found it a nerve-wracking ordeal.'

Leanne's mother, Sharon, left the kitchen door unlocked for three months hoping that her missing daughter would sneak back home at any given moment. 'I kept thinking that she might have lost her key or forgotten which one was for the back door, so I left it open to allow her access to the house around the clock. After a few months had passed I realised it was foolish to leave the house unsecured, especially during the night, and reluctantly I started to lock it again.'

Despite the emotional pleas from her family and the reconstruction, no one came forward with any reliable information about Leanne and Det Supt Gregg was becoming increasingly concerned. 'It was looking more and more likely that she had been taken against her will. The route she had been expected to take was almost a mile long and wound through an estate of around 7,000 residences.

The initial search involved 200 officers a day using a variety of methods, including helicopters, mounted police, trained dogs, underwater search teams and forensics to systematically search the area.

Detectives had to ascertain fairly quickly who lived in the vicinity and their first port of call was to look at people whom they knew had a background of sexual offending, as that was the most likely motive for Leanne's abduction. Secondly, they had to conduct a thorough fingertip search of Houghley Gill to try and unearth any shred of evidence that Leanne had been there. There were 42 drains in the Gill alone and they all had to be checked in case she had been placed down one of them, dead or alive.

Gregg feared that Leanne had succumbed to the

clutches of a murderer. 'The time Leanne walked through the Gill it would have been totally dark as there was no lighting there. It is a sinister place enclosed by trees and shrubbery, but I think Leanne had used it many times, despite advice from her family to avoid it. Houghley Gill is surrounded by houses and is a high risk location for an abduction because it is so overlooked. However, it was looking more and more likely that that was what had happened.'

Forensic psychologist, Dr Richard Badcock, was convinced that Houghley Gill was the place where Leanne's kidnapper had snatched her from. 'The track is frequented by plenty of residents so there's a good supply of potential victims passing through. By taking a position near the top of the Gill you can see who's coming from both sides. This means you can choose a victim and still see whether you are likely to be interrupted by anyone else.'

Gregg was concerned that Leanne's attacker was also watching every move the police made during the investigation very closely. 'We were mindful that if somebody local was responsible for abducting and murdering her then they might well dispose of her body in an area that they knew we had already searched, so we had to inspect them all again. We even had to examine old maps to pinpoint hidden wells in the area that would have provided an ideal hiding place for a body.'

Detectives knew from interviewing Sarah that Leanne had stepped off the bus at Stanningley Road, near to the junction with Houghley Lane. She then left Sarah and walked alone along the lane to Houghley Gill. From there she would have worked her way up through a densely populated area known as the Musgraves towards her home in Landseer Mount which was approximately a mile away. The journey should have taken her a maximum of 20 minutes.

Police called the route Leanne was expected to walk home the Red Route and searched around a thousand residences along it in the first few weeks of the hunt. Leanne's sister, Michelle, was touched by the willingness of the community to throw open their doors to strangers. 'It was nice to know so many people cared. Not only did they join in the hunt for Leanne, they also never complained when the police thoroughly searched their houses. It meant a lot to us.'

When local houses yielded no further leads, detectives dredged the canal and searched railway lines and a nearby industrial complex for her body.

The underwater police team struggled to see their hands in front of their faces as they painstakingly searched five miles of the Leeds-Liverpool canal. For a two-mile stretch, water levels were lowered to one metre to allow a fingertip search along the murky canal bed. The River Aire, which runs through Bramley alongside the canal, also posed problems. It is a wide, fast-flowing river and the fierce current made a thorough examination difficult. During the search for Leanne, specialist assistance was drafted in from British Waterways, the British Transport Police, the Ministry of Defence aerial reconnaissance department, Calder Valley Search and

Rescue Team, the National Missing Person's Helpline, other police forces, Interpol and the National Search Team Centre. It took several weeks to complete the detailed search, but still nothing of significance was found.

It looked like the teenager had literally vanished into thin air and the police were coming under mounting pressure from the media and the community to find her. 'We still don't know for sure at what point she was abducted, but we feel confident that the most likely place was from Houghley Gill' Gregg told journalists. 'Time is critical in a case like this. The first 36 hours are crucial as they are the prime period for finding someone safe and well. As the days go by our concern for the safety of the victim increases and, of course, the anxiety rises for the family.'

During the investigation police found mobile phones, telescopic umbrellas, carrier bags and items of clothing that they suspected could belong to Leanne. Forensic examinations and identification by members of her family proved that none of these items belonged to the missing schoolgirl.

The search for Leanne Tiernan soon became the biggest missing person hunt in the history of West Yorkshire Police. The search took in 800 sheds, garages, outbuildings and commercial premises in a half mile radius from where Leanne was last seen alive. Telephone companies were enlisted to help trace her mobile phone, which had been activated the day after she disappeared.

A local businessman pledged a £10,000 reward for

information leading to Leanne's safe return and the supermarket chain, Iceland, featured details and a photograph of Leanne on cartons of milk sold in 760 of their nationwide stores.

Forensics examined Leanne's bedroom, removing her schoolbooks, toothbrush, bedclothes and other personal items to obtain her fingerprints and build up a DNA profile that might help during the investigation. The police also collected 300 samples of DNA from people they interviewed and later cross-referenced the samples to eliminate any suspects from their inquiries.

Detective Supt Gregg was particularly interested in the information supplied by four female witnesses. 'One lady told us that she had see someone fitting Leanne's description walking alone through the Gill at the time of her disappearance. We still don't know whether it was her or not. Two women who live near to Houghley Gill reported hearing a loud scream followed by silence around the same time.

'And another lady came forward to report that she had seen a middle-aged man in Houghley Gill walking his dog an hour before Leanne vanished. She recognised him as someone she had seen loitering in the Gill for the previous three weeks.' Despite appeals for him to come forward, and attempts by the police to catch him on covert surveillance cameras, they failed to trace the man. It later transpired that this suspect was indeed the person who had abducted and killed Leanne.

Gregg appointed two family liaison officers to support Leanne's family throughout the investigation: 'As the weeks went by we began to fear that Leanne had probably been murdered and we had to gently broach the subject with her parents. It was a very difficult conversation but we had to prepare them for the worst outcome. They refused to accept it. Each of them said, "No, we've got to remain hopeful that she is alive and will be found safe and well, because we can't carry on if we believe that she is dead." '

In a desperate attempt to find her, Leanne's parents even combed the red light districts wondering if she had been lured into prostitution. Sharon would rather believe that Leanne was working as a hooker than accept that she might be dead. 'We thought she may have been kidnapped and given drugs and then sent out onto the streets to earn enough money to fund her addiction and a pimp.'

Even Det Supt Gregg was beginning to wonder if he had missed a vital lead. 'As a police officer it haunts you 24 hours a day. You are constantly asking yourself the question: "where is she?" You're always wondering if you have missed something obvious that will lead you to the answer.'

To help broaden the hunt Gregg consulted experts at the National Crime Faculty and the National Search Centre to seek further advice on how and where to search for Leanne and to build psychological profiles of likely offenders.

Forensic psychologist, Dr Richard Badcock, believed that the kidnapper had spent months planning the abduction. 'He probably used an approach that would take the victim by surprise with force, maybe threatening her that he had a knife. He would be thinking about how he was going to control the victim and plan how he would get her out of the area and to where the main offence would take place.'

The police hadn't uncovered anything that suggested a struggle had take place in the vicinity where they believed Leanne had walked home. And this lack of evidence fuelled the family's hopes that she had run away rather than been abducted. Sharon was convinced that Leanne would return home for Christmas, but the festivities came and went and still there was no sign of her.

'I spent days adorning the house with Christmas decorations to make it welcoming for her, because I felt sure she would walk through the door on Christmas Eve. We waited and waited but she didn't show up. Then my mother thought she would turn up for Christmas dinner, so we prepared a huge feast that none of us really wanted to eat and sat at the kitchen table waiting for her to stroll in demanding her meal. We didn't want to face the fact that she might be dead. It was like giving up on her and she had only been missing for a few weeks. I even started to wonder if she was pregnant and was too afraid to tell me.'

Her close friend, Sarah Whitehouse, wasn't convinced that Leanne had run away. 'I didn't believe she had just disappeared like that, because if she was planning to run off she would have told me about it. She would have confided in her best friend that she was unhappy at home and was planning to get away for a bit. She might even have asked me to go with her. Although she was a confident person I don't think she would have had the guts to run off on her own without telling somebody about it.

'Leanne was the funniest, most outgoing person you could ever have met. She was like a ray of sunshine, always bright, happy and laughing.

'We were incredibly close and when she went missing it was like a part of me had gone too. We used to do everything together and suddenly there was no one there any more. I will never have another friend like Leanne. She is irreplaceable. I think about her all the time and wonder what she would be like now. I've changed such a lot since she disappeared. As time went by I became increasingly withdrawn and unhappy, to the point where I hardly went out any more.'

Another close friend of Leanne's, Sammy Lee, has equally happy memories of her, 'We had a favourite song called "Friends Forever" and it was our theme tune because we pledged that we would be friends forever. The summer before she was kidnapped we went on holiday to Turkey together and that is the last really happy memory I have of her. It's one I will always cherish.'

While her friends accepted that Leanne might be dead, Michael Tiernan clung to the desperate hope that she was still alive and was prepared to listen to anyone who supported his belief. 'No matter what, I never allowed myself to believe that Leanne wouldn't be found alive. We had clairvoyants ringing us up saying that she would be found in the woods but they always insisted that she was alive. It gave us hope. One even said that she had run away with a red-haired boy and gave us an address in

Hull where they might be. We went to Hull to look for her but, of course, she wasn't there.'

The weeks slipped by and three months after Leanne's disappearance Sharon reluctantly returned to work and tried to restore some normality to her life. Her world had been turned on its axis but she knew that for her own sanity she had to carry on with life. 'My employers were very understanding and I comforted myself that Leanne knew where I worked and if she did come home she would know where to contact me.

'For the next few months my life was a hazy blur of going to work, coming home and going to work again. It was really hard for my other daughter, Michelle, because I was so focused on Leanne all the time that I didn't really give her the attention she deserved.

'I was always looking for Leanne, whether I was on the bus to work or wandering around the shopping centre. Sometimes I thought I'd spotted her but then on second glance I would realise that it wasn't Leanne.'

On her first day back at work Sharon walked to the bus stop in a daze, oblivious to the inane chatter of other commuters discussing their day around her. The bus pulled into the stop and Sharon boarded. She felt isolated. Detached from the rest of the world, she stared intently between the shoulder blades of the person in front of her, waiting for the queue ahead to pay their fare and move over.

She edged forwards, holding out the exact money – and froze. Leanne's smiling face staring cheerfully at her. 'Where to love?' the driver prompted her. 'Er, what? Er, sorry!' she replied, taken aback by the imposing appeal poster pinned up next to the driver. She hadn't expected to see posters of Leanne. Did other people on the bus know she was her mother? Were they pointing at her, wondering if she was a bad parent whose child had run away? Sharon handed over her money and sank into her seat, burying her head from prying eyes.

'It was such a shock to see her face on that poster that I was completely immobilised and speechless for a few seconds. I got used to it eventually but until the day her body was found I never stopped looking for her.'

After months of believing that Leanne was dead Sarah Whitehouse began to wonder if Leanne had run away after all. 'Five months had gone by and there was no sign of a body so I started to think that maybe Leanne had run off and I didn't know her as well as I thought I did. I was convinced that if she had been murdered then the police would have found her body by then. So I kept my mobile phone permanently charged and switched on just in case she tried to get in touch.'

Weeks after Leanne vanished, a television news bulletin reported that the body of a 16-year-old had been discovered in Nottinghamshire, just over an hour's drive from Leeds. The report said that the teenager had been fatally stabbed and Sharon rang the police, fearing it was Leanne.

'The family liaison officer reassured me that it wasn't her but every time something like this happened my stomach lurched. Shortly afterwards a female body was found in a nearby river and again I thought it must be my daughter. It was torturous.'

Nine agonising months after Leanne had vanished, seemingly without trace, Det Supt Chris Gregg received an unexpected phone call. 'I was told that a female body had been found about 16 miles from Bramley at Lindley Woods in the Washburn Valley. My instinct told me without a doubt that this was Leanne. I went to Harrogate District Hospital to attend the postmortem and as soon as I saw the body I knew that it was Leanne Tiernan. She was wearing a distinctive eyebrow ring and her hair was still tied in pretty much the same way as her mother had described. We had to formally identify her using fingerprints that we had taken from her schoolbooks, but that was really just a formality. It was the end of our search for Leanne and the beginning of our hunt for her killer.'

Every inch of Lindley Woods was scoured for evidence that might lead the police to her murderer and Det Supt Gregg launched an appeal asking for information on anyone with connections to Lindley Woods. 'We felt it was important to focus people's minds with that particular question because we were sure that it was no coincidence that her body had been dumped there. It was a well considered location.

'I sent a detective inspector and one of the family liaison officers to break the news to Leanne's family and prepare them for the bombshell. Once she had been formally identified I went to speak to her parents personally and explained to them that we believed Leanne had been strangled. They sat and listened in a state of shock and horror and the pain they must have been experiencing at the time is unimaginable.'

For Sharon Hawkhead the news was a strange mixture of relief at finally learning what had happened to her daughter and plummeting despair at the crushing knowledge that she would never return home. 'The day Leanne's body was found I was at work and the family liaison officer telephoned me to say that a body had been discovered at Lindley Woods. At that point they hadn't identified the body and it was just a courtesy call in case we heard about it on the news. Later that day he called me again and said they needed to come and see me. The penny dropped and I realised that this time it must be Leanne.'

Earlier that day Michelle had experienced a sixth sense that Leanne would soon be found. 'I woke up that morning and I just couldn't stop crying. I was filled with grief and couldn't understand why I felt so dreadful on that particular day. I walked downstairs and was overcome with such sadness and anger that I started to peel the kitchen wallpaper off with my fingernails. I had no idea at that point that she was about to be found, but subconsciously I must have sensed it. I was so distraught I had to take the day off work. It was like I'd been hit by a tidal wave of grief.'

Later that day Michelle visited her father's house to give her younger stepbrother, Jack, his birthday present. 'While I was there my mother called and insisted I go over immediately because the police were on their way and she feared it was going to be bad news. I went straight over and found my mother hysterical in the garden, looking out for the police car.' Michelle gently ushered her inside the house and tried to calm her before the police arrived.

Sharon had already assumed the worst and was wondering how she was going to break the news to the rest of the family. 'Strangely, I remember my most prominent thought was how was I going to tell Leanne's grandparents. My father had had a stroke a fortnight earlier and my mother was stressed trying to care for him. I just couldn't imagine how I was going to tell them.'

Det Supt Gregg explained how they had identified Leanne by matching her fingerprints to several items they had retrieved from her bedroom in the days following her disappearance. Sharon sighed deeply. 'Are you looking at suicide or murder?' Gregg replied: 'Definitely murder. We believe she was strangled.'

The words rang in Sharon's ears. 'I couldn't take it in. This sort of thing happens in films, not to ordinary people like us in Bramley. Michelle was shaking and staring at the floor and we just didn't know what to do with ourselves. We had waited nine long months for news of Leanne and now we had it we were lost for words. Our hopes of her ever coming home were completely shattered.'

'Can we see her?' Michelle asked between sobs.

'I'm afraid not. She has been dead for a long time and her body has been exposed to the elements,' Gregg replied softly.' It would cause you more distress if you viewed the body and we have to carry out a number of forensic tests to try and detect who killed her.'

Michelle nodded. 'At least now we knew she was dead, we could start grieving. Our biggest fear was that it was someone we knew that had murdered Leanne. We kept wondering if her killer was somebody we had invited into

the house; if we were to blame in some way for introducing them.'

Leanne's father, Michael Tiernan, was travelling home
from Sunderland on the day she was found. 'The police
told me that a body had been discovered but it hadn't
been identified yet. There had been other bodies but I had
a feeling that this time it could be Leanne. When I
arrived home a draft blew the newspaper open on the
kitchen table. It fell open on a page with an article about
the body in the woods. It was like a sign to prepare myself
for the bad news. Although it is devastating to have your
worst fears confirmed there is some comfort in finding
out, because it allows you to move on rather than clinging
on to false hope.'

After months of following the story the media turned
to the family for their comments. Sharon told reporters: 'I
can't put into words how I'm feeling today. It's just the
worst possible news. We've been living in hope since she
went missing that she was still alive. We were praying
that this was not Leanne. She was a lovely girl. She was
my baby. She was my mate. I just miss her so much.'

Leanne's closest friend, Sarah Whitehouse, echoed the
sentiments: 'I feel like I'm in my own little world and
none of this feels real. My best friend is dead and it feels
like a nightmare.'

Although the family couldn't view the body Det Supt
Gregg arranged for them to visit the place where Leanne
was discovered in the woods. Sharon found it difficult to
accept that Leanne had been dumped there. 'My visit to
Lindley Woods was strange. The police organised a car to

take us there and we were warned that the press would want to take photographs of our visit. I couldn't relate to the woods as being Leanne's resting place before her funeral. I couldn't imagine that she had been lying there. I've never felt any connection with the place or had the urge to go back.'

A couple of days before the funeral, Leanne made her final journey to her family home. Sharon felt comforted by the timing of her arrival. 'The funeral directors brought her back just after 5 pm, which was the time she was due to come home the day she went missing. I finally felt like she had come home and completed her journey.' The family sat with the coffin and the next day, which would have been Leanne's 17th birthday, they raised their glasses and proposed a toast to her.

Sharon involved Leanne's friends in the preparations for the funeral at Sandford Methodist Church in Bramley and requested that people wear bright colours rather than black.

'We decided we wanted the funeral to be a celebration of her life rather than a mournful occasion, because Leanne was always so vibrant and cheerful. Even so, the day was hard to get through.'

Sister Janet Durbin, the Deaconess who led the service, reflected on how the 16-year-old had been cruelly snatched from her family when she was on the brink of adult life: 'Leanne was a normal, happy, fun-loving teenager, half child and half young lady.'

Leanne's sister, Michelle, was one of the pallbearers carrying her white coffin. 'We wanted to make sure that only women carried the coffin. Her last experience in life had been a terrifying ordeal with a man and the women wanted to carry her coffin to her final resting place as a mark of respect. There were a lot of people paying tribute to her with beautiful speeches and it was a very touching ceremony. I think the hardest part of the funeral was having had her home, we then had to deal with letting her leave the house again and being stuck somewhere cold.'

Leanne's best friend, Sarah Whitehouse, was also a pallbearer. 'It was so hard carrying that coffin knowing that my best friend was lying inside. It was such a hard day to get through. There were so many tears shed.' Sharon's most testing moment was selecting flowers for the funeral. 'Choosing flowers for your own daughter's funeral is the hardest task in the world. You know that they are going to sit on her coffin and it just brings it all home to you. It's hard to come to terms with losing your child. I still go to the cemetery every week and take fresh flowers. It's my way of feeling close to her.'

Sharon has since moved, but she often spends her quiet moments holding Leanne's duvet cover which still bears the holes cut out of it for forensic examination. 'I imagine how she used to look when she was curled up in bed. She was always cold and I used to have to rub her back to warm her up. Those memories keep her alive and close to me.'

While the family tried to come to terms with their bereavement, detectives were working around the clock to find Leanne's killer. During the manhunt Michelle developed a growing distrust of all but her closest friends and family: 'We had to deal with the fact that her murderer was still at large and no one had any idea who he was. I felt like I couldn't trust anybody. I would walk past complete strangers in the street and stare at them, wondering if they were responsible for her death.'

Det Supt Chris Gregg surveyed the evidence: 'There were a number of items left on Leanne's body that proved to be of vital importance to us. They offered investigative potential that we knew could lead us to the killer. The area where Leanne's body was found was in the heart of a dense wood. The grave had been partially dug and her body dumped on the surface. We believed that Leanne's killer had taken her body into the woods with the intention of burying her, so why hadn't he?

'Archaeologists told us that the ground was spongy due to the thousands of pine needles shed from the conifers and the trees were planted very close together, creating an entwined root formation. This meant that it would have been extremely difficult to dig very deep. So the likelihood is that he had probably started to dig and when it became difficult he abandoned the project and just left the body there.'

A woman contacted the police and told them that she had been driving past Lindley Woods at midday exactly a week before Leanne was discovered and noticed a man lifting a bundle of floral rags out of a car boot. She wondered if he was planning to dump them in the wood and particularly remembered the distinctive floral pattern of the duvet cover. Gregg was convinced that she had witnessed Leanne's murderer disposing of her body.

He instructed forensics to take a closer look at the duvet cover. It was badly stained and covered in dog hairs. There was no manufacturer's label on it, but the pastel floral design suggested it wasn't contemporary and that the owner had probably had it for a number of years. Closer examination of the dog hairs was later to provide another clue to the killer.

Gregg drafted in a highly skilled team of experts to examine Leanne's body and the scene of her final resting place. An entomologist assessed the insect growth in and around her body, while a botanist studied the vegetation growth on the corpse to determine how long it had been deposited in the woods.

Gregg also called in a specialist forensic scientist to identify the pollen on her body and the items she was wrapped in to provide them with clues to the premises of the killer.

Medical experts surmised that her body was not as decomposed as they would have expected and suspected that her corpse had been stored in a freezer. Police sought advice from the Centre for Cell and Tissue Research at York University to examine the possibility. Dr Ashley Wilson, a specialist in patterns of ice-crystal growth in frozen items, was called in to determine from the texture of the tissues whether Leanne had been frozen in a domestic or industrial freezer.

'I visited the pathologist at Sheffield Coroner's Office and was supplied with a sample of Leanne's body tissue. I looked at the internal structure of the tissue and the muscle blocks and looked for damage that may have been caused by a freeze and thaw cycle.

'As water freezes it causes damage to the tissue. Water is lost from the cells as the ice-crystals grow and the cells are forced apart causing considerable damage to the tissue structure. When the tissue is thawed the damage remains. There was consistent damage that confirmed that she had experienced at least one slow freeze and thaw cycle in a domestic deep freeze. Further tests ruled out that this could have been caused while the body was placed in the woods, as the temperatures were not cold enough.'

A criminal psychologist believes that her killer had developed an obsession with her corpse and returned to the deep freeze repeatedly to look at it: 'He would have got more pleasure from the victim once they were dead because he developed a fascination with the body. Although Leanne didn't appear to have been sexually assaulted the killer would have achieved sexual gratification from the murder. A certain degree of aggression will compensate for sexual failure and develop into sado-masochism. Then the interest gradually shifts from voyeurism to personal contact and the greatest satisfaction comes from strangling. The sensation of the physical contact with the victim substitutes for a sexual experience.'

The criminal psychologist believes that the reason the killer had later disposed of the body in the woods was either to make room for another victim or because his domestic freezer had broken down and he couldn't be bothered to replace it.

Although there were several items worth closer examination, experts never found any of the killer's DNA on
Leanne's body or at the scene. However, on the back of
her sweater the forensic pathologist discovered a small
half-twist of burgundy carpet fibre and detectives
realised that if she had been murdered in a house, then
there was a strong chance that the carpet was still there.
Gregg was keen to keep a lid on the evidence. 'It was
something we couldn't afford to get into the public
domain. We knew that if we got into the right house and
the carpet was still down, it would be a vital breakthrough for us.'

Pathologist, Dr Kenneth Shorrock, confirmed that
Leanne had died from ligature strangulation. When her
body was found she still had a cable tie and a grey scarf
double-knotted around her neck while her hands had
been bound behind her back by using three cable ties, one
around each wrist and then another used to link them
together. The police were keen to find out where the cable
ties had been sourced.

Detective Constable Nick Dodsworth was part of the
team drafted in to identify the manufacturer of the cable
ties. 'There were three types of cable ties found on
Leanne and each tie had its own symbol that identified
the manufacturer. We sought outside assistance to help
us trace them. We discovered that the type used to bind
her hands was manufactured in Italy and had only one
distributor in the UK, who supplied mainly to Royal
Mail. Clearly we had to focus our attention on who would
have access to these.'

The grey scarf that had been double-knotted around Leanne's neck revealed on closer examination a number of human pubic hairs lodged between the fibres. Scientists set about extracting a DNA sample from the hair to see if they could find a match in police files.

Gregg was determined to investigate every possible lead, no matter how inane the evidence appeared to be. Leanne's body had been encased in several green plastic bin liners that had been tied with twine and placed inside the floral duvet cover.

Dr Richard Badcock felt the number of bags used offered clues about the personality of Leanne's killer. 'The number of bin bags she was wrapped in seemed excessive compared to what was required to carry the body safely to the woods. It suggested something excessive in the offender's make-up. It was a demonstration of control and containment and that again suggested that the motivation was sexual.'

Detectives contacted the British Plastics Association to help them ascertain whether there was anything unique about the plastic bin liners. It was an inspired move. They discovered that the liners were 40 microns thick and because of the distinctive perforation and striation marks they were able to trace them to a company in Stockton-on-Tees in the North East, who manufactured them exclusively for Morrison's supermarkets. Gregg was amazed that such an everyday household item could help them narrow down their search.

'We knew there were Morrison's supermarkets near to Bramley, where Leanne lived, so it suggested to us that the killer had links with the area. When her murderer was finally arrested we found a chard of identical bin liner plastic attached to a nail on one of the floorboards upstairs which provided us with another piece of incriminating evidence.'

The other significant item police discovered on Leanne's body was a dog collar that had been used to secure a plastic bag over her head, and there were also a number of animal hairs found on her.

The scientist who examined the hairs believed they were a blend of dog hairs and could belong to more than one animal. Gregg sanctioned some groundbreaking work with forensic scientists in America to extract DNA from the dog hair in a complicated scientific process. Peter Grant from Wetherby Forensic Laboratory and Detective Inspector Martin Hepworth travelled to the USA to meet Professor Bob Dunston at the Department of Veterinary Pathology at the A and M University in Texas. It is the only department in the world able to extract DNA from a single animal hair and it was the first time that a dog's DNA profile was obtained for a British criminal case.

Detectives tasked with tracing the dog collar secured around Leanne's neck identified the manufacturer as Armitage Leather Products in Nottingham. They invited the managing director of Armitage to view the dog collar and he confirmed that it had been produced by his company.

To corroborate this, scientists counted the stitches and measured the distance between the puncture holes and rivets to confirm conclusively that it was an Armitage product. The collar had only been made available to the retail market a year prior to Leanne's disappearance. The company's distribution network was international and detectives set about the tedious task of tracing customers who had purchased the collars.

There were a number of outlets in Leeds and around 200 retail and wholesale outlets throughout the country. Few shops retained customer records but nevertheless Gregg's team contacted all 200 outlets to enquire whether they had details of customers from Leeds.

They contacted a company called Pets Pyjamas in Liverpool who relied mainly on Internet and mail order sales. They checked their records and revealed that they had a customer in the Armley area of Leeds who had purchased six identical dog collars by credit card a month before Leanne disappeared. He was called John Taylor and Armley is the neighbouring district to Bramley, where Leanne lived. It was a major and unexpected breakthrough.

Detectives ran John Taylor's name through their computer records and discovered that a female had telephoned them with his name, following their appeal for information about people with connections to Lindley Woods. She claimed she had met John Taylor through the lonely hearts adverts and he had taken her to Lindley Woods and the nearby Sun Inn public house. She told police he had confided in her that he used to go poaching in the woods as a child and was familiar with them. Chris Gregg had a hunch that they were on the right track:

'Clearly this man was emerging as an interesting character who we needed to speak to urgently.'

Taylor didn't have a criminal record and the only details the police could find in their own files was a complaint he made several years earlier about a broken window. However, the supplementary detail listed his occupation as a delivery driver for Parcel Force, which is affiliated with Royal Mail. Could this be someone who would have access to the exclusive yellow cable ties? Detectives paid him a visit at his workplace in Bradford. He claimed he didn't know Leanne and denied any involvement with her disappearance. Undeterred, the police sent a forensic team to search his house in Cockshott Drive, Armley, the following week. Sifting through the squalor they unearthed vital and compelling evidence that linked him to the crime.

Clad in pristine white coveralls the forensic team slowly worked their way through the debris and over-turned furniture littering the floor and grubby work surfaces. Animal hair, grease, dust and dirt shrouded each room and a stale odour hung sickeningly in the air.

Gregg was astounded by the squalor that Taylor lived in: 'His house was a complete mess. He'd separated from his wife and lived alone for several years and seemed to have let his hygiene standards slip considerably. The place was in chaos and needed a good clean throughout.'

All the carpets in the house had been removed but minute strands of burgundy carpet fibre were still attached to the nails on the floorboards and there were burned sections of identical carpet hidden in the rear garden.

Under closer examination they provided a perfect match to the twists of carpet fibre discovered on Leanne's sweater.

Forensics also found samples of the rabbit netting twine Taylor had used to tie the green plastic bin liners encasing Leanne's body. And a tiny chard of green plastic matching the bin liners was recovered from a floorboard nail upstairs.

Carefully forensics removed broken cable ties from the garden fence posts and matched them to the ones used to bind Leanne. Inside the house every surface was thickly blanketed by dog hair, some of which didn't scientifically match the single dog owned by Taylor. But when a team of archaeologists excavated the back garden and unearthed a burial ground it became clear what had happened to the other animals.

Thirty ferrets and a number of dog carcasses were discovered in the small plot and the forensic team doubted that many of them had died from natural causes. They retrieved the buried corpse of a black and tan Border Terrier and took it to a veterinary pathologist to determine the cause of death. It was confirmed that the dog had died from a severe blow to the head and police believed that Taylor had savagely beaten the dog with a meat cleaver.

The animal matched the description given by the lady who saw Taylor walking a dog through Houghley Gill an hour before Leanne's disappearance. Detectives were convinced he had destroyed the dog because it provided vital evidence that could lead a trail back to him.

The police knew they had considerable evidence but

before they arrested John Taylor they paid a visit to Sarah Whitehouse: 'The police showed me a photograph of him and asked if I knew who he was. I said no, I've probably seen his face around the area but I don't know him personally. When they had arrested him they told me that he lived nearby to my house and I went cold because I realised that he had probably seen Leanne and I walking around several times before he actually pounced on her. It could so easily have happened to me. I used to walk through Hougley Gill and he could have followed me at any time.

'People have told me that the bushes have since been cut back in the Gill and that it is much more open than it was, but I've never been there since Leanne went missing. I will never walk through that place again. It holds too many unpleasant memories. I still remember that the last words I said to her were, "See you later," and I can still picture her walking away from me.'

Gregg and his team started to unravel Taylor's background. He was 46 years old and was born at Hyde Terrace Hospital in Leeds in 1956 to Margaret and Frank. He was the eldest child and had a sister, Angela, and a brother, Michael. He attended Castleton Primary School in Armley and continued his education at Armley Park but he was an unremarkable student and left at 15 with no qualifications.

He took a number of short-term unskilled jobs and in 1977 he married nursery school teacher, Janet Tyson, who was also a leader and member of the Girl's Brigade. They met at Armley United Reformed Church where Taylor was an officer in the Boy's Brigade.

The couple had two children, a boy called Andrew in 1980 and two years later their daughter, Alexandra, was born. In 1983 they moved from their home in Elsworth Street, Armley, to a three-bedroom terraced house in Cockshott Drive, where he would later murder Leanne. Here Taylor began a new career buying and breeding dogs. He built several kennels in the garden and began making his own rabbit nets to sell through the local newspaper.

Janet began to tire of the animals running around her once pristine home and fouling the now flea-ridden carpets. By 1994 Taylor had added two owls to his collection, which he fed on one-day old chicks that he bought in bulk orders of 2,000 and stored in the family freezer. Local residents nicknamed their oddball neighbour Pet Man.

Janet walked out on Taylor and the couple divorced in August 1996. A year later he placed adverts in contact magazines and travelled around the country to meet the women who replied. Detectives analysed Taylor's telephone bills and began to trace the women he had met to question them about the nature of the relationship they had shared with him.

DC Dodsworth was involved with the project: 'We managed to identify at least 25 women who had shared some sort of a relationship with Taylor. It was embarrassing for these women because we had to ask them some very personal questions so that we could build a profile of Taylor's sexual appetite and tastes. From our interviews it became clear that he was highly sexed and manipulative.

'The majority of women described him as an unkempt,

unusual, rather odd person, particularly regarding his sexual preferences. Some of the women only met him a couple of times, yet he still managed to have intimate relations with a lot of them. He didn't appear to be targeting a particular type of woman, although he did develop an interest in a young girl.

Just a few months after kidnapping and killing Leanne, remorseless Taylor attempted to lure 15-year-old Donna Exley to his home for sex. Donna's mother was a friend of Taylor's and he used his association with her mother to try to achieve intimacy with the teenage girl.

Donna soon sensed that John Taylor wasn't quite what he appeared to be. 'At first he seemed quite friendly, but the first hint I got that he was putting on an act was when my five-year-old sister cracked a harmless joke at his expense and he snapped at her. She called him Postman Pat because he worked for Parcel Force and he told her in no uncertain terms that she must never call him that. He didn't have any sense of humour.

'When my brother offered to clean his car for him John insisted that he wasn't allowed to go near the boot and kept checking on him all the time. He hated anyone going near his car or touching his things.'

But worse than a lack of humour, Taylor had his sights set on Donna Exley to satisfy his deviant sexual urges. 'On the first night I met him he waited until my mum had left the room to put the kids to bed and he put his arm around me and was trying to cuddle me and touch my leg. It wasn't appropriate. I kept shuffling away from him and begging him to stop, but he wouldn't. Then when my mum came back in the room he acted as though nothing had happened.

'He used to call my mother and if I answered the telephone he would start talking about how he was going to come around and tie me up with handcuffs and whip me or he would ask me to get into the bath and play with myself. He would say things like, "Hi sexy. I'm wearing nothing and I've got a whip in my hand ready to whip you." He told me he preferred teenage girls to women and kept asking me to wear skirts to show off my legs.

'He invited me to stay at his house and said that he could give me a better time sexually than boys my own age. He told me not to tell my mum and got quite angry with me when I kept refusing to stay with him. I made it clear that I was never going to go, but I think that if I had I would have been his next victim. It got to the stage that whenever he came round to the house I avoided him and hid in my bedroom. He made me feel sick and nervous from head to toe. It was horrible.'

Donna suffered in silence for weeks, until her mother paid Taylor a visit at his own home and saw a different side to him. 'Eventually my mother went to his house and she realised what he was like. She went upstairs to use the bathroom and because there weren't any doors on any of the hinges she noticed that the bedroom was full of whips, handcuffs, ties and nipple clamps. She spoke to his neighbours who told her that he had women coming in and out all the time.

'She said the house was dirty and untidy. There were dog hairs everywhere, even in the oven, and that there were no carpets down and all the doors had been taken off the hinges. She couldn't understand why he chose to live like that. Now we know that Leanne's body was hidden in the house somewhere at the time, probably in the freezer. It doesn't bear thinking about.'

DC Dodsworth knew that Donna Exley could be a key witness if Taylor persisted in his not guilty plea when he stood trial. 'It was of great importance that only a matter of months after abducting and killing Leanne, here we have Taylor trying to seduce a 15-year-old girl to have sex with him. It demonstrates the lengths he would go to, to satisfy his urges. He described to her in explicit detail what he would like to do with her and she was still a very young girl.'

After Taylor's conviction Donna recalled other signs of Taylor's questionable behaviour.

'There were times when he went away for weekends and told us that we couldn't call him or send him text messages. I've often wondered what he was doing during those weekends away. When I found out that he had been charged with Leanne's murder I realised how close I had come to being his next victim. I felt sorry for Leanne's parents and ashamed that I had even known him.'

During the investigation police interviewed a 34-year-old woman who had shared Taylor's home in Cockshot Drive only months before Leanne had disappeared. Single mother, Deborah Benjamin, had lived there with Taylor and her two teenage children after meeting him through a lonely hearts column.

'I placed an advert in the newspaper describing myself as a blonde with hazel coloured eyes who enjoyed the outdoors. John Taylor replied and we arranged to meet in a café. He seemed charming and he took me and my kids out for a lovely day on the Whitby coast.'

They started dating and Taylor gradually introduced her to his world of hunting and poaching and took her to his favourite haunt, Lindley Woods. She described to the police how he was heavily involved in buying, selling and breeding animals and how he devoured every moment he could spend game shooting, rabbit hunting and fishing in Lindley Woods.

'A few weeks after we started dating he asked me to move in with him. We were getting along really well so I agreed but after a couple of months he started to change and became very demanding. He insisted I wore more skirts and blouses and become more feminine.'

By this time Taylor's home was like a miniature zoo. He shared it with two Alsatian puppies, seven Border Terriers, 28 ferrets, one polecat, 40 chickens and a duck. Deborah described how one day when one of the puppies attacked the duck, Taylor shot it and then went on to kill all the chickens and hang them up in the kitchen with bags over their heads.

'The house was filthy. When I moved in I really had to scrub the place clean. One room was locked all the time where he kept the dogs. The stench was awful because it was full of their mess.'

Gregg carefully read Deborah Benjamin's statement about Taylor's lifestyle. He pieced it together with earlier findings of butchered animal remains buried in the back garden. 'Taylor appears to be an ordinary man but he is not. He has an extremely dangerous nature and this is displayed in the way he has treated animals throughout his life.'

Although concerned by John Taylor's behaviour towards animals, what disturbed Deborah most was his sadistic sexual appetite and deviant demands in the bedroom. 'The sexual side of his nature was sickening. He got his kicks out of being sadistic and tying people up.

'He loved bondage and kept cable ties in his drawer in different colours and lengths. They were at hand when he needed them. He wouldn't stop even though I kept saying it was hurting.

'It makes my blood run cold when I think about it. He would strap both my arms and ankles to the bed and blindfold and gag me. I went along with it because I thought everyone did it. He was really excited by it. One day he disappeared for a few minutes and then came back with a cherry tree branch from the garden and started whipping me with it on the inside of my legs.

'The next time I told him I didn't want to be strapped to the bed so he tied my hands behind my back using cable ties and then tied one around each of my breasts, pulling them really tight and hitting them with the cherry tree branch. I was screaming with pain and yelled at him to stop. He only stopped when he saw me crying.'

Another woman told police how he had bound her hands and breasts with cable ties in the same way and a female referred to during the trial as Miss D revealed how Taylor had told her he enjoyed 'kinky sex', tying women up and locking them in cupboards. Deborah ended her relationship with Taylor after four months. Just two months later he developed another fantasy – to pursue schoolgirls. He spent weeks looking for a suitable victim and eventually snatched Leanne Tiernan from the desolate Houghley Gill wasteland.

Deborah had demonstrated to police how Taylor had secured her hands using the cable ties during their bondage sessions. The configuration she described was a perfect match to the method used to bind Leanne Tiernan's hands behind her back. DC Dodsworth reported back to Gregg. 'We knew without a doubt at this point that we had the man who had abducted and killed Leanne.'

Michael Harding also had suspicions about Taylor. He had been visiting Lindley Woods since childhood. He joined the boy's brigade when he was nine years old and used to go camping in the woods about 200 yards from where Leanne's body was found. John Taylor became an officer in the Boys Brigade when he was 18 and he took Michael Harding, then aged ten, for a day of rabbit and fox poaching in the woods.

Harding was horrified by crazed Taylor's blood lust. 'We cornered a young fox and let the hounds loose, but instead of letting the dogs finish the job Taylor grabbed the terrified writhing animal by its hind legs and gored it to death with a knife. When I heard about the murder I joked to my wife that he might be responsible. There was something sinister about him that set him apart from the rest.'

The police learned more about John Taylor's extreme methods of slaughter when they were contacted by a poacher. He told them he was sickened by Taylor's violent antics. He recalled how one night he and Taylor had set out to kill a sheep.

'Taylor just drove at the sheep and hit its back end. Its head hit the door and it fell into a ditch. He climbed out and put it into the back of his car and took it home. The next morning he carried the sheep up to his bathroom where he skinned and gutted it.

'John Taylor could go out poaching alone from dawn till dusk and he had this way of vanishing. I'd be walking along the railway line and he would be walking towards me and then he would just turn and disappear. He never seemed to catch much but when he did catch a rabbit he revelled in inflicting pain, killing and mutilating it. Now I wonder if half the time his mind was really on looking for his next victim and any rabbits he caught were just a bonus.'

Gregg was beginning to get the measure of Taylor: 'In my view he is a very cool, calculating individual. He is a hunter and a poacher by nature. He led a nocturnal life and his movements over the last few years have been difficult to track. He's a person who is isolated and has few friends. He had a string of jobs but in 1998 he began working as a delivery driver for Parcel Force where he would have had access to the cable ties. He has been married and had grown-up children and was living a life which, to the outside world, appeared to be fairly ordinary, but in reality it was anything but.

'We spoke to many of his family, friends and associates

and discovered that he had lived in Bramley and Armley for most of his life. He had worked on market stalls selling pet foods periodically and travelled widely to satisfy his love of poaching, hunting, fishing and meeting women. This was a person who had a sinister and secret dark side to him.

'We managed to piece together a great deal of what we considered to be overwhelming evidence. Not only forensically, but also about the sexual practices he enjoyed and, in particular, the bondage with the cable ties that he used in an identical configuration to the way Leanne had been tied. This, to us, was compelling evidence that he had abducted her.'

Finally Sharon Hawkhead would no longer have to wrestle with a faceless demon. She would learn the identity of the man who had mercilessly killed her daughter. 'The police were very good at keeping us informed. When he was a suspect they showed us his photograph and asked us if we knew him. We didn't and I was relieved about that. At least we weren't responsible for introducing him to her. It was a random selection. After they had searched Taylor's house and arrested him they told us that he had confessed to kidnap but was denying murder.'

Gregg knew it was only a matter of time before Taylor would crack and confess the true nature of his crime. 'When we first arrested and interviewed Taylor he had days to think about it. He knew that we had a forensic team in his house and that we would find compelling evidence that he killed Leanne.

'He was desperately attempting to deflect the impact of a cold blooded, well-planned kidnap and tried to suggest that he was out walking his dog when events overtook him and he allowed himself to get carried away. We believe he had been waiting for weeks for a potential target and he was there with the sole intention of abducting a young female.'

Det Sgt Dave Wilson interviewed Taylor: 'He was quite scruffy and had a certain odour about him. He smelled of cigarette or pipe smoke. He was trying to be affable and friendly and made a number of admissions, but they were only partial admissions. He was trying to put himself in the best position to minimise what had happened.

'He claimed Leanne had brushed past him and before he had had time to think it through he turned around and grabbed her, instructing her not to scream. He says he stifled her after she emitted one scream, then he tied her hands behind her back with his dog lead, placed his coat over her head and frogmarched her over half a mile to his house. The walk would have taken around 22 minutes and this poor girl must have been out of her mind with fear.'

He claimed that when they reached his house he forced her upstairs to the bedroom where he removed her coat and bound her with cable ties. He recalled that her mobile telephone started to ring and he demanded to know how to turn it off. Fearing for her life, she told him which buttons to press. The call was undoubtedly her mother, Sharon, desperately trying to contact her.

Taylor confessed he was in the process of cutting up

some jeans to make a hood to conceal his identity when Leanne's blindfold slipped. He claims he lunged at her to cover her eyes and a struggle ensued and she fell to the floor, sustaining a fatal blow to her head.

He insisted that believing she was dead he left her in the room and returned the next day to wrap her in bin liners and place her in the garden under some wooden pallets. He told police he later moved her back inside and stored her in a compartment below his sofa until he decided to transfer her to Lindley Woods. Taylor denied ever keeping her in a freezer.

Sharon Hawkhead was furious that John Taylor had not disposed of Leanne's body earlier. 'I'm quite angry about the length of time that he kept her. He held her body for nine months before abandoning her remains in the woods and we could have been put out of our misery a lot earlier if she had been found sooner.'

When police questioned Taylor about the cable ties and the scarf double-knotted around Leanne's neck he claimed he had put them there after she had died. His defence counsel, Graham Hyland QC, told the court at his trial that he was no longer maintaining that account and that he admitted that he knew that Leanne was not dead at that point.

Taylor had also insisted during police questioning that the day he abducted Leanne, November 26 2000, was his first trip to Houghley Gill and that he had been there to search for his missing dog. Detectives were later able to disprove this when a woman selected him from an identity parade as the man she had seen walking his dog on the day Leanne was kidnapped and had noticed in the Gill several times during the three weeks prior to Leanne's abduction.

But despite the mounting evidence, Taylor refused to acknowledge that he had premeditated Leanne's kidnapping and murder, leaving the police with the onus of proving he was the guilty as charged. 'We felt it was important to be able to demonstrate to the court the true extent of what happened to Leanne that day, rather than John Taylor's version of events. We had to prove to the court beyond all reasonable doubt the true callousness of a crime we believed he had planned with meticulous detail. Taylor stuck rigidly to his account until the trial, when he was faced with overwhelming forensic evidence and he finally changed his plea to guilty.'

The change of plea stirred mixed emotions amongst the family. Sharon was relieved that he had confessed but felt cheated of an explanation of the way her daughter had died. 'The fact that he'd decided to plead guilty to murder at the last minute was annoying because he escaped having to explain what he had done. I was hoping to have a lot of questions answered in the courtroom. We have never found out what he did with her boots, her coat, the presents she bought for Sarah or her mobile phone.

'He told the police that he had dumped them in the river, but that isn't true because the phone was still receiving signals for several months afterwards. I can never have her back but I would like to have her things back. Instead we are still as much in the dark today about what happened to her as we were when she first went missing. We will never really know the full circumstances of her murder.

'I would like to know why he picked on Leanne that day. She wasn't dressed provocatively. She was wearing black trousers and a baggy coat. She wasn't looking for trouble. She just wanted to get home out of the rain, in time for her meal. I've always liked to think that she was in the wrong place at the wrong time, but the police seem to think that he was lying in wait for her; that maybe he had seen her before. We didn't have much in life, but Leanne, Michelle and I always had each other. Why of all people did he have to pick on Leanne?

'It was weird coming face to face with him in court. I had imagined him to be a monster and I was struck by how ordinary looking her was. I had a morbid curiosity. I wanted to see what Leanne would have seen and heard. I still can't believe that someone so average managed to drag away my daughter and kill her. I know there is no way she would have gone with him willingly. She would have kicked out, scratched and screamed, unless he threatened her with a knife and she was so terrified that she complied with his demands.'

Det Supt Gregg believes that Taylor admitted his guilt at the 11th hour for his own self interests: 'By admitting his guilt he avoided having to really say what went on in the house and as he left for Wakefield prison to serve two life sentences he took his dark secrets with him.'

Robert Smith QC, prosecuting, told the court that Taylor's conduct bore distinct similarities with the sexual activities he had engaged in with consenting women. He revealed that Taylor may have assaulted Lianne: 'Given the condition of Leanne Tiernan's body when examined it is impossible to say whether or not she had actually been sexually interfered with.'

Graham Hyland QC, representing Taylor, told the court: 'John Taylor was unable to give any explanation to the police as to why he committed this dreadful crime and regrettably that remains the position today.'

When sentencing him the judge, Mr Justice Astill, told Taylor, 'Your purpose, whether you can recognise it or not, in kidnapping this young girl was so that you could satisfy your perverted cravings. You are a dangerous, sexual sadist and this was a premeditated encounter. You were in the area for a purpose. It was not an act of impulse.'

He added that Taylor had deliberately disposed of her body in a way that meant that it was not found for months, subjecting Leanne's family and friends to unimaginable agony while they waited to find out what had happened to her.

Leanne's sister Michelle sat in the court and listened in horror as the evidence unfolded: 'Hearing some of the things that he did made me realise that he is not a person, he's a demon. When the judge summed up Leanne's case he just sat there shaking his head as if to say: "I didn't do that." It was dreadful.'

After Taylor was led away Sharon Hawkhead told waiting reporters, 'I am pleased that he has been locked up so he can't do this to anyone else or put another family through what we have had to endure. We hope that in this case life really does mean life.'

But life for Sharon Hawkhead will never be the same again. 'I have lots of little things to keep Leanne's memory alive. I have artwork she did for me when she was a small child and I have my memories of her. Because she died when she was 16 she will always be a child to me. I will never have the pleasure of knowing her as an adult and seeing her married with her own children.

'She's the first thought that pops into my mind in the morning and the last thought in my head at night before I go to sleep. I talk about her whenever I can. John Taylor has taken away half of my life. Michelle is one half and Leanne was the other half.'

Her father, Michael Tiernan, cherishes his memories of his youngest daughter. 'I will always remember the great times I shared with Leanne. She had a beautiful smile and the most sparkling eyes. Even now when the stars are out at night we go out and say that Leanne is smiling down at us with her twinkling eyes. We always associate the stars with her. When I think of Leanne she will always be the energetic teenager who loved a good party and was always on the go. Sometimes I wonder what she would have been like as an adult and how her life would have developed.'

For the police, John Taylor's trial and sentencing was by no means the end of their inquiry. Det Supt Chris Gregg felt Taylor might have the blood of other victims on his hands: 'We consulted criminal psychologists and they concluded that Taylor had probably committed other offences. It was unlikely that he had reached the age of 46 and then decided to commit an offence of such gravity.'

They reopened their files and looked at crimes that had taken place in the vicinity where Leanne had been abducted. There was an unsolved incident dating back to October 1988, some 12 years before Leanne's murder. A woman had been raped but her attacker was never found. With the advances of science police were able to forensically prove that Taylor was the rapist. They still had an item of clothing and slide samples of semen from the investigation and were able to prove with DNA evidence that there was only a one in a billion chance that the attacker could have been anyone other than Taylor.

The woman had been walking alone through Houghley Gill and was attacked by a balaclava-clad man brandishing a knife. It was a particularly vicious attack in broad daylight. He dragged her up the bank into the bushes and raped her at knifepoint.

At that time, despite a huge police investigation, the person responsible escaped prosecution. Taylor had no previous form and was completely unknown to the investigation team.

The victim told police: I was walking to school to collect my daughter and decided to cut across Houghley Gill. I had only taken four or five steps when I was grabbed from behind. During the struggle I noticed he was wearing a balaclava. He pulled out a knife and ordered me to lie down on the ground and he raped me at knifepoint.'

The Houghley Gill rape in 1988 bore similarities to a rape four months later in 1989 when a woman was attacked in her own home on the nearby Broadlea estate in Bramley. She was in her kitchen when she sensed a presence in the room. A man had entered through the unlocked rear door, wearing a balaclava. 'He had a knife and even though my daughter was crying he persisted and started to take my cardigan off.' He forced her upstairs and subjected her to a brutal rape after blind-folding, gagging and binding her.

Taylor tried to distance himself from the area by faking a Geordie accent and claiming that he had visited Bramley specifically to attack her. Before he left he told his victim that he travelled to different parts of the country to rape women and said he was going to board the train and do it again to someone else in a different area. He revelled in terrifying and controlling women.

Four months after Taylor was imprisoned for life for Leanne's murder he was brought out of jail to face more questioning about the rapes. Both women described the man as wearing similar clothing and having a North East accent. Taylor denied throughout a series of inter-views that he was the rapist and even gave an alibi for the time the house attack took place, claiming he was at the Waterloo Cup hare-coursing event in Southport.

Faced with overwhelming and condemning DNA and circumstantial evidence Taylor pleaded guilty to both charges of rape. On 4 February 2003 Taylor was sentenced to a further two life sentences. The judge said they were two of the most serious rapes he had ever dealt with, describing them as violent and depraved in the extreme. Psychiatric reports revealed Taylor was a sexual psychopath unable to control his aggressive sexual impulses and the judge stated that Taylor was a danger to any woman he came into contact with.

On hearing the news, Michael Tiernan said, 'For Taylor to rape two women years before he murdered Leanne, he must have known what he was capable of before he abducted her. I don't think he has shown any remorse and I believe to this day there are a lot of things he has kept to himself that we will never get to know about.'

Sharon sat in court to hear the verdict: 'As I listened to the evidence I started to think that Leanne was lucky she died before he managed to do the things to her that he had done to the other two women. That's a sad conclusion for any parent to have to arrive at.'

The police continued to re-examine their files and returned to Taylor's home to look for clues to other crimes he may have committed. They removed the floorboards of his bedroom to check for traces of DNA of other victims he may have killed there.

An undetected murder they felt could have links to Taylor was the death of prostitute Yvonne Fitt. In 1992 her stabbed body was discovered in Lindley Woods, buried 200 yards from where Leanne was found. Had Taylor already buried his dark secrets once before in the woods and returned nine years later to bring another victim to his secret burial ground?

Gregg was keen to investigate the link: 'Was it just coincidence that two female bodies turned up in the same woods? We've got to look carefully at this particular crime and make sure that if there is any evidence to connect Taylor with this incident, then we look into it.'

Psychologists believe there could be a link: 'The method of killing isn't what interests Taylor, so although Yvonne was stabbed and Leanne was strangled it could still have been done by the same person.'

Yvonne had been working as a prostitute in Bradford when she disappeared and, like Leanne, her body was found nine months later in Lindley Woods, 12 miles from where she was last seen alive.'

Detectives also still wonder if he was linked to the death of 17-year-old Deborah Wood whose burning body was discarded on the embankment of Burley Park Railway Station in 1996. Emergency Services were called to extinguish a fire and when they arrived they discovered the body of a young woman had been set alight. Again, there were similarities with Leanne Tiernan's murder. Like Leanne, Deborah's body had been wrapped in plastic bin liners and bedclothes and the corpse appeared to have been frozen.

Deborah lived alone but was close to her father, Peter Woods, and had been with him in the hours prior to her disappearance. 'On the day she went missing we had walked into town and done some shopping and then we called at a pub for a few drinks. Some of Deborah's friends came in so she decided to stay on for a while after I left. She promised to call me later when she got home but never did.

'I knew there was something wrong after I hadn't heard from her for a couple of days. It was unusual for her not to call me. We spent a lot of time together playing cards and dominoes and it was rare for a day to go by when I didn't hear from her. I went to her bedsit to see if she was at home and when there was no reply I asked her neighbours if they had seen her. They told me that they hadn't seen her for a few days and I really started to worry.'

Deborah's mother, Linda, was the first to hear that her daughter had been brutally murdered. 'I saw the story on the local news and the report mentioned some red gloves found on the body. I knew then that it was Deborah.'

Linda formally identified Deborah from the remains of her clothes that didn't perish in the flames. Dental records and DNA taken from Linda and Peter Woods also confirmed that the victim was their daughter. Peter Woods was first notified of Deborah's death by the police. 'I was hysterical when they told me that she had been murdered, stored in a cold place for a while and then the killer had poured petrol on her and set her alight. She was such a wonderful daughter and her death is a huge loss to me.'

The contents of Deborah's stomach suggested that she had died within 24 hours of leaving the pub and pathologist Chris Milroy said there were indications that she had died from asphyxiation.

The police have never found Deborah's killer, but the strong links with Leanne's murder lead her parents to believe that John Taylor could be responsible. Senior investigating officer on the case, Andy Brown, says: 'There are no cast iron links to Taylor but it certainly could have been him. There is no conclusive evidence but there is certainly a lingering suspicion.'

One item that still baffles police is a silver necklace set with pink stones discovered in the boot of Taylor's car: 'We found it trapped under the rubber boot seal and have never been able to trace who it belongs to or how it got there. It could belong to another victim,' says Gregg.

Taylor is serving four life sentences and Judge Justice Astill recommended that he never be released from prison. Det Supt Chris Gregg and his team continue to re-examine their files to see if Taylor has any connections with any other previously undetected crimes.

'I don't believe he has ever shown an ounce of remorse for what he has done to any of those women. There could be other people whose lives have been affected by him. We will work as long and as hard as is necessary to uncover any other offences that he has committed. No stone will be left unturned.'